Christmas
2005

to the Birkinshaws
whose influence is notably
evident throughout this book

Why State Schools Fail

Why State Schools Fail

And what can we do about it?

Jill Clough

With a foreword by
Jilly Cooper

UIT CAMBRIDGE LTD.
CAMBRIDGE, ENGLAND

First published in England in 2005.
UIT Cambridge Ltd.
PO Box 145
Cambridge
CB4 1GQ
England

Tel: +44 1223 302 041
Web: www.uit.co.uk

10 9 8 7 6 5 4 3 2

13-digit ISBN 780954 9 452919
(10-digit) ISBN 0-9544529-1-7

FOREWORD
by Jilly Cooper

Jill Clough is the most delightful, warm, wise, intuitive person. I state this categorically in case teachers and educationalists from the maintained system pick up this book and think, "Why is this stroppy cow from the independent world attempting to tell us how to put our house in order?"

Jill — in fact — had a dazzling career as a head in several independent schools but because she wanted to give something back and help really deprived children, she changed careers and went to Brighton in an attempt to rescue an almost terminally failing state school. This is the story of her valiant battle and how despite all her efforts she was unable to prevail against the powers of educational darkness and bureaucracy.

Jill writes with great humility and, in the end, both sadness and anger because she believes, like all good teachers do, that children matter first and that all children, however deprived their backgrounds, should be given a chance in life to succeed. I would advise anybody who cares about education to read and consider this touching and important book.

Bisley, Glos.

Editor's Note

East Brighton College of Media Arts, the school this book relates to, finally closed as a secondary school in the summer of 2005. The building may be re-used for other educational purposes.

Contents

Chapter 1

Why I am writing this book

I took up the post of Principal, East Brighton College of Media Arts, in January 2001. The school is adjacent to the Whitehawk estate, which has a long history of social problems. It had been placed in Special Measures — a term used by inspectors when they judge that a school needs direct supervision by Her Majesty's Inspectors and additional resources from the local education authority, for a period of about two years. It had already been closed in 1999, after several years in Special Measures, and had re-opened under its current name as a new school, under a provision called 'Fresh Start.'

I am writing this book because I discovered that I could start the process of regeneration but also that I could not continue the process without the real cooperation of the city as a whole. I discovered that the underlying structures, emotions, systems and moral assumptions of our society, exemplified in this city, work against such schools and their students.

I am not alone in this discovery. Staff who had joined East Brighton College of Media Arts from other parts of the country rapidly came to find themselves both pitied and praised by teachers in other schools. This was to make sure that the staff at the school would in some way 'contain' the students, making sure they did not leak into other schools because they were perceived as so dangerous. Conversely, Derek Bown, the chair of governors, often remarked that he detected in those working in the local New Deal for Communities a subtle desire to maintain a state of failure so that the 'doing of good' could continue. Everyone needed the school to exist, because deprived children 'deserve' their own school.

Education is a powerful tool for social engineering, which is why politicians see it as a prime focus for their activity. However, in responding to those who elect them, they endorse the elitism which is still a hugely powerful element in our class structure. Bruce Reed and John Bazalgette, of The Grubb Institute, in a paper written in 1976 (for Shirley Williams, when she was Secretary of State for Education), entitled *Education for Mature Responsibility*, defined elitism as 'the building up of a social class which considers that it has the right of access to, and control of, the values which dominate a society'.

The sensitivity of the associated issues is acute. We see it in arguments about grade inflation in school-based examinations. It is perceived that too many students gain A grades at Advanced level; or too many young people acquire first and second class degrees. We do not have enough failures to satisfy everyone that standards are secure. We seem to need, as a society, to be engaged in a perpetual redrawing of boundaries between those who are acceptable and those who are not. At the same time, we are required to become inclusive, by exhortation, rather than through real understanding of our own impulse to repel those we do not like. From playground excluding of children who smell 'wrong' to adult statement 'If I wanted my child to sit next to someone from the council estate I would have lived on the estate', or to inflated house prices nearby so-called 'successful schools', we have created a vicious circle which makes sure that those who are born on the outside stay there. Everything inside the current education system is framed by our politicians to make sure that they will be re-elected: on the one hand, seeming to give 'equality of access to all' and on the other hand ensuring that outsiders remain outside, just so that 'high standards' can be vindicated. By definition, in our society, high standards cannot be universally achieved (see above: grade inflation).

My experience is not unique but it is rare, in that I spent most of my career in independent schools. Few headteachers have moved from independent schools to state schools. My experience spans attending garden parties at Buckingham Palace, because of the status of one of the schools I led, to standing with an education welfare officer at the doorway of a house to try to persuade a student to come to school. Behind the neat front door there was a kind of wasteland.

In one school, there was a parent who as a managing director of De Beers was trying to raise funds to educate poor black children in South African townships. In the other, there was a parent who sat across the table in my study and said to his thirteen-year-old son, sitting on the other side of it, 'I don't fucking want him. He's doing my head in. I'm going down the Social to tell them they can take him. He's not coming back to my house.' Tears rolled down the face of the child.

I have been angry for a long time now: I cannot get rid of the emotion, although I am not an angry person by nature. I have learned to understand the major factors that produce this stark and terrible contrast. I know that other people understand them too. I struggle to make sense of my personal experience of trying to reconcile the differences, and my discovery that there is huge, hidden emotional resistance to setting right the problems which give rise to the contrast. I have always believed that, in the end, people want the best for others; but this experience has severely challenged that faith. I wonder if I am just naïve.

Although the current Government has set about changing some of the basic assumptions, by insisting that 'every child matters', the reality is that little will change until we own up to our apparent need for *scapegoats*. We are willing for children to grow up into angry, dysfunctional and distressed adults, living at the margins and permanently excluded from the more joyous experiences that our society can provide. We have known for a very long time what we do to create and sustain the conditions in which children grow up damaged. It took centuries before the Children Act in 1989 actually acknowledged that children have rights. There may be more legislation to change the way in which as a society we manage the development and education of children; but until there is a real change of heart about who takes responsibility for whom — until we can all say, 'I am my brother's keeper,' and act accordingly, estates like Whitehawk will continue to flourish.

Chapter 2

Buildup

I went to the post as a very experienced head. Educated at a girls' grammar school in Bristol and the University of London, I went straight into school teaching because I half-thought I was filling in a year before going into research. I loved academic work and wanted to be a university teacher.

But I loved teaching in schools. The work in which I engaged for my PhD helped me to grasp the relationship between feeling and culture, and gave me a framework for thinking about schools. People are over-impressed by academic qualifications; the value of my research was not the higher degree itself, but the rigour of the process. I learned to sense disinformation; even where I knew little or nothing about a subject, I could tell whether or not I was being given reliable evidence. I learned, too, to think systemically: in practice, this means that if people do not achieve what they ought, or behave badly, I look first at the system in which they work. Has it been established primarily to help them succeed, or is it constructed to keep them in their place?

My first headship was in the independent sector, at The Royal Naval School for Girls, Haslemere (now known as The Royal School). The Queen is the Patron and senior members of the Ministry of Defence are among its governors — for instance, the

Commandant General of Marines — although there is nothing at all military in the school. I spent eight years as headmistress, and in the course of that time learned much about leadership, not just for myself, but also in industry, the City and the armed forces. I was deeply involved in promoting the academic advantages of single-sex education for girls, through the Girls' Schools Association. I ran the first national conference for Head Girls, met and worked with influential figures in leadership teaching and development, met the press, appeared on television, talked on radio. I trained with Ofsted (the Office for Standards in Education) to inspect independent schools and was part of several inspection teams. I held a short schoolteacher fellowship at Christchurch, Oxford, to investigate gender issues in education and reviewed books on gender issues in leadership.

In 1995, at the age of 50, I became the headmistress of Wimbledon High School, one of the Girls' Day School Trust (GDST) schools and expected to stay as head until my retirement. There could be no more rewarding or exciting school to run. I loved the culture of commitment to social justice, and the tolerance of eccentricity.

In 1996, I was elected to the Council of the Secondary Heads Association (SHA), and began to work with headteachers nationally. For instance, I represented SHA in the early consultations about the founding of the National College for School Leadership. I co-wrote several books with fellow heads, and was invited to run training and development seminars for SHA. I reported to the Council of SHA on the leadership and management advantages of leading independent rather than maintained schools: primarily, the clear accountability. Dame Angela Rumbold was chair of governors, and shared cheerfully her experience of being Schools Minister.

Whilst at Wimbledon High School I felt the attractions of working inside the network of GDST, which attracts expertise at national level to work with its headmistresses — partly through its network of high-achieving and well-placed alumni. Given the imperatives of the market place, the heads are given freedom far beyond anything in the maintained sector. I could choose professional development of a really demanding kind, in particular through working with The Grubb Institute. The Institute brings together the social sciences and theology, in order to analyse and understand the dynamics of how people behave inside organizations, and although its work is not publicized, it has been highly influential for forty years. Members of the Institute have provided advice to the judiciary, politicians, the public health sector, the prison service, and a multitude of organisations both nationally and internationally. Among its more striking activities was writing the paper which underpinned the Good Friday agreement in Northern Ireland, and providing advice on factors which generated the Brixton riots. More recently, on behalf of the Department for Education and Skills (DfES), the Institute has trained Behaviour Education Support Teams in about 90 local authorities. I was invited to join the Council of The Grubb Institute and am now a member of the core staff.

In 2000, I decided that I wanted to work in the public sector, where the need for clear thinking about education is most acute. I believed that I understood how to help individual children to achieve highly, and with confidence: through child-centred education — seeing through the eyes of the child. I learned this by working with the country's most privileged children, and their parents. I had no illusions about either. I was naïve, though, in assuming that other people wanted as passionately as I did the success of children who are brought up in poverty and deprivation.

The Royal Naval School, Haslemere

I became headmistress of The Royal Naval School (RNS) — a boarding and day school for girls founded by naval officers after the Napoleonic Wars when they were on half-pay. They assumed that their sons would go to sea, but that they would be unable to provide dowries for their daughters who would therefore need to work.

Plainly, with the cuts in armed forces, the school population was only loosely connected with the Royal Navy when I arrived.

Most were either the daughters of stockbrokers and the like, living in Haslemere, or were international. It was not a culture in which I was comfortable: there was too much money, too many well-founded assumptions that the future would be relatively easy to map out.

At the same time, the market was very tough for small girls' boarding schools — despite its name, the school was not well known in the RN, and I discovered that I had to take marketing very seriously. I set out to make the school known and to discover how to increase its market. First of all, I tried to understand its background and the assumptions and expectations of current parents and governors.

With the Queen as Patron, there were royal occasions aplenty. I went to Royal garden parties, enjoying the dignified queuing outside Buckingham Palace, the sightseeing queue, the ushers in their morning suits marshalling the ranks, the scrambling queue for tea. It was all far more democratic than I had imagined because of the wide range of people invited; but it exuded privilege. Everyone invited had been identified and chosen by someone with influence. When the Queen came to visit the school to open a new building, ranks of other dignitaries arrived because that was the protocol. The Queen enters a county and the Lord Lieutenant must be there to greet her. The strength and intricacy of this culture amazed me. I was taken to Horseguards' Parade for the Trooping of the Colour; the Royal Box in the Royal Albert Hall for the Mountbatten Festival of Music; dinner with Admirals in the Painted Hall in Greenwich. My chairman of governors (by then the Governor of Gibraltar) introduced me to the Duke of Edinburgh, just because he could. I had dinner in the Mansion House in the City of London, where someone was inducted into a Livery company. I went to sea on an aircraft carrier and arrived there in a Sea King helicopter. The School Choir sang in Westminster Abbey, St Paul's Cathedral and on the BBC World Service.

Through the above experiences, amongst others, I gradually felt the power of the social networks that run through the lives of those who work in the City, in the armed forces, in international corporations, in the media. I never felt comfortable with such networks, not just because I did not come from them myself, but because I was deeply uneasy about how we educate the privileged. Nonetheless, I tried to believe that by educating the daughters of influential City brokers and bankers, and other social leaders, I could encourage them take responsibility for their own lives and to develop social conscience. The service ethos of the RN and Royal Marines was what I chose to build on, in order to try to reconcile the huge power of wealth and social connection with the influence that others and I might have simply through our own education.

That influence would be used to try to create the same opportunities for those without the social networks as for those whose lives were wholly framed by them. I learned to believe that every time an adult says, 'I was useless at school,' someone, somewhere in education, ought to be cringing. Every day, fantastically successful human beings make fools of educationalists because they have grown up resilient and mature despite the education system.

The governors had strong views and were used to authority. Some were Ministry of Defence appointees, coming to terms with major defence cuts, peace-keeping and introducing women working at sea on equal terms alongside men. The Commandant General of Marines was automatically a governor, as were the Chaplain in Chief, the Director of the Women's Royal Naval Service (WRNS — until the WRNS were phased out), and the Chief Naval Appointer. One governor was Comptroller of the Navy, in charge of procurement. An ex-merchant banker, also a governor, said regularly, 'Education is our business.' There were other headteachers as governors, too. Their collective approach was formidable. I had to learn fast to keep their respect and understand their priorities. I discovered that my own role was to educate them about schools so that they could make the best decisions.

Enormous resources of intelligence and ingenuity were now available for me, and I set out to learn from and exploit whatever I could so that the pupils at the school could have rich opportunities. When I saw young recruits training at Britannia Royal Naval College, Dartmouth, and the Royal Marines on Dartmoor, pushing themselves to physical and mental limits, I developed a healthy respect for the power of individual determination, regardless of other people's estimate of that person's talent. I also realized that the capacity to manage physical risks well was one which needed to be developed, if girls were to become intellectually as well as socially confident women.

The grounds of the school were full of trees. From the high branches of some were hung ropes on which the pupils could swing. These were favourite places. In my first term, the Bursar — ex Naval Captain of the old school — rushed to tell me that a girl had 'come off' the ropes and broken both elbows. He wanted me to ban the ropes from being used at once.

I thought carefully and fast, and did not. On investigation, it proved that the girl had not 'come off', but been flung off during one of their games — a posse of girls at the end of the rope swinging it round as hard as they could. I thought it was a predictable accident but an allowable risk. I would doubtless have taken part myself as a child. As an adult I swung on the ropes myself when no one was about. The risk was in the behaviour, not in the presence of the ropes. We could try to change the behaviour so that swinging on ropes was within acceptable limits. The Bursar was troubled at the thought that a pretty girl might end up with a facial injury. I thought of the sundry scars I had accumulated in playing hockey and cricket as a schoolgirl.

The parents were sensible and supportive. Alison completed her education at the school, elbows duly healed.

The role of the head is to provide the model for leadership and learning for the entire school community. You create the conditions and define the language to be used. You need to be physically close to and engaged with the whole community. All your actions have symbolic value, however slight.

Every school has 'the worst year group ever'. I thought this attitude was commercial suicide, not an allowable assumption, and tried for a couple of years to change the behaviour of one particular cohort, together with the assumptions of the staff, but with limited success. Then I discovered that my secretary's husband was a Brigadier in charge of a local army 'command and assault' course. We could use it, with army physical training instructors (PTIs) as advisers. The entire year group and many of their parents and brothers came too. Girls who thought they were 'best at sport' had to cope with seeing shy but suddenly agile peers swarming across the high rope strung above a tank of water. Brothers showed off and fell in.

The best moment came from a simple game. A large square, split into three rows of three, was chalked on the ground and eight girls were issued with the first eight letters of the alphabet randomly sorted. Each girl had to stand in one square. Their instruction was to sort themselves into alphabetical sequence only making the approved moves — that is, not diagonally. All moves had to be negotiated, of course; and I had been asked to select for the task some of the most difficult girls.

We stood rapt as they struggled with the concept of cooperation. A little Japanese girl with embryonic English jumped up and down in excitement in her square. She could see exactly how to solve the puzzle, but the others were too busy quarrelling to pay attention. The PTI took me aside to make his comment *sotto voce*: 'They won't defer leadership, will they? Everyone wants to lead.'

This observation changed the entire way in which we managed the year group. They went on to become highly successful.

The more I listened to parents, the more I wanted to understand and learn from their experiences. I found my way on to senior management training with ICI (as it then was) and to other similar opportunities. My own professional development evolved not so much through educational training of the kind now promoted for headteachers as through business and commerce.

I needed to understand the culture of the governors, too. I learned how one of the country's major institutions operates, visiting the Navy's major training and development establishments, including the Maritime Tactical Centre, where industrialists went to see war games played in order to develop their own business tactics.

For six years I sat on the Admiralty Interview Board, helping to select the graduates who would go forward for training as officers. This was a wonderful opportunity to sit in the seat of employers, looking at school and university records and references and assessing the sense young graduates were able to make of their education. They had critical problems to resolve. I had to subsume my own judgement to that of the Board. It was an excellent discipline.

I began consciously to use the insights I was gleaning about how apparently unpromising individuals have great inner potential: society needs all the talent it can get, never mind the label. I started looking for explanations and discovered the work of Howard Gardner, Harvard Professor of Education and of Neurology at Boston. He had defined intelligence as 'multiple' rather than just what was conventionally assessed. I looked at everything we provided in the school — both in the formal curriculum and in extra-curricular activity — to see if these many kinds of intelligence were identified, encouraged and assessed.

I was, of course, free to work in this way. I had to account to the governors for what I thought because it had to make business as well as educational sense; but I had tried to understand, articulate and refine the underlying beliefs of governors and parents alike.

In effect, parents and governors between them provided professional development for the headteacher of their school because they saw how this would contribute to the improvement of the school. I found the best development for myself from sources outside formal education, and perhaps this gave me sympathy with what many of my pupils seemed to want, too — freedom to choose according to their own strengths and needs.

Students with apparently low cognitive ability can still do very well at public examinations if studying subjects which reflect their home life and experience. Somehow, they absorb the vocabulary and concepts with their mother's milk. Working with individual strengths may mean working with the family experiences; so why differentiate between family predisposition to business and commerce and family life focused on water-skiing?

One pupil developed epilepsy at about the age of fifteen, and her confidence and aspirations were severely dented as a result. But she found herself in Advanced level Business Studies. Both parents were astute business people and she had listened to their conversations for as long as she could remember. She succeeded academically, as well as learning to live with epilepsy.

Building the capacity for pupil leadership became a very high priority — it was a development from helping pupils to teach one another. I learned not to rely on my own assumption about leadership, either.

It is possible to be highly effective as a leader without being highly articulate. The ability to speak confidently in public does not in itself imply or confer leadership qualities. A prefect was elected as head girl by her peers. She often found it very hard to tell me what she meant, and shrank from public duties which involved speaking to an audience. But her peers trusted her — she had plenty of courage. She gained sponsorship for her degree course in engineering; and later, at university, won an award for leadership as well as a first class degree. Her communication was excellent, even though words were not her instrument.

Once you engage with the whole school community in this way, you discover, too, that you have to lead and manage whole-school emotions, such as grief. One year, several parents and staff seemed to be afflicted with cancer; one after another died and the level of shock was profound.

I realized that I needed to make explicit these underlying feelings — not just finding vocabulary myself, but making links between people so that they could handle the emotions themselves. We had a very skilled school chaplain, and I drew on his strengths. What interests me in hindsight is that although there were plenty of agnostics and other faiths in the school, too, they all felt it was proper that the head should be explicit. I am a Christian and although I do not find it easy to talk in public about this, I know that there are times when the fact that I believe matters a great deal, even if I am surrounded by agnostics or those with different faiths. It meant that these terrible events were given their due weight.

This faith also framed all my other assumptions: about human potential, primarily. If you believe that everyone is uniquely valuable in the eye of God, everything you organize in a school stems from that conviction. Always support dreams generously. Overestimate.

One pupil passionately wanted to become a vet. Conventional ability tests showed that she would probably get Advanced levels but not the top grades necessary. I tried to warn her and her parents, in case they were all disappointed. Crossly, she went to another school and did outstandingly well. Her determination was overwhelming. I was wrong.

The trouble starts when schools and society become snobbish about the kinds of talent they are willing to commend. I learned, here, that too often when pupils are disruptive we start making moral judgements about behaviour instead of looking truthfully at the systems in which we require them to work. Pupils are just as capable of being intensely bored and unhappy in independent schools as in maintained schools; and for similar reasons. What is different is the freedom as well as the responsibility to resolve the problem. No child can be allowed to fail.

In my time at RNS, I learned at first hand about privilege: about how children born into families that are secure either financially or emotionally make assumptions about their lives which become self-fulfilling. I learned about the business of education, alongside tough and high-achieving governors; and I learned about the market.

In my first week as a head, a parent came to tell me he was moving his daughter to Marlborough School, because the school was now opening its doors to girls aged 13 and above. 'No criticism of this school,' he said, ' but I want her to have my advantages.' Marlborough had been his own old school. It was impossible to explain to him that girls in single-sex schools are far more likely to choose science and maths Advanced levels than those in mixed schools; they choose what they like, not what they are expected to choose. He carefully explained to me that I must first 'sell to your own'. I learned fast and uncomfortably that marketing is not about reality but about perception, which is located in memory, images and assumptions not easily reached.

Although one of my own daughters spent six very happy years in the school with me; although public examination results improved markedly; although we developed strongly as a staff; still the school had to contend with the vagaries of the market. After the collapse of the stock market in 1990, we then had to work within the shrinking market for boarding.

Boarding, I discovered, was a very powerful tool for improving behaviour, in spite of the adverse publicity given by men who had bad experiences at public school. Girls who behaved outrageously at home, or who struggled because of their parents' equally outrageous conduct, found school to be stable, secure and encouraging. They could start to build up memories of time spent in peace; activities without stress; relationships which were trustworthy; experience of justice; gradual slackening of resentment. They were also spending time with pupils who loved boarding school and chose it. Joy in the process was infectious. Children who might have been damaged were able to rediscover that life could be normally enjoyable and constructive. They learned to deal better with life.

Wimbledon High School

In 1995 I moved to Wimbledon High School (WHS). Instead of having fewer than 300 pupils, I was now in charge of almost 900, including an attached primary school. WHS is a member of the Girls' Day Schools Trust: affiliated to another twenty-five schools all over the country. Places there are highly valued. Instead of wooing prospective parents, I was trying to explain why there were no spare places. Response to the market in the independent sector means that you do not expand a school just because it is popular and successful — the very factors that make it good are likely to be related to its size.

GDST schools are largely urban, mainly formed from direct-grant girls' grammar schools and now wholly independent.

They are governed by a single council with executive powers, and supported by a central administration with its own personnel, legal and property departments. Each school has its own set of local governors, with influence rather than authority. This occasionally causes the local governors some frustration since they are usually exceptionally able people, but they find they must defer to the central decision-making of the council and its time-scale. They do, however, have the casting vote in the appointment of the headteachers. Members of the council are impressive — Baroness Warnock has only recently retired, for instance. It was impossible for me not to feel excited by the chance to talk to her: she continues to influence both the education and medical systems, through her report on Special Education, her Committee on human fertilisation and embryology, and her current thinking aloud about the ethical implications of euthanasia. Far from being remote from the day-to-day business of managing schools, she spent six years as the headmistress of Oxford High School.

GDST has a powerful network of women who have attended the schools. Wimbledon alumni include Oxford and Cambridge university professors as well as distinguished professionals in many fields. The other strength of GDST is that it is itself a network of schools, none of them unduly large, all having attached primary schools, all with some striking characteristics in common.

At WHS, my task was primarily to identify what was good and to ensure that it was embedded, so that the school would continue to be responsive to its market. With a highly-educated and articulate parent population, most of whom had considerable idealism, opportunities to try out the best of educational strategies were abundant. One of my main tasks was to make sure that parents knew as much as possible about what actually happened in the school. Rumour had it that the school was an academic hothouse, and yet many parents chose it because it was not. There was reasonable scepticism about academic results, alongside the expectation that they would be excellent, of course. The pupils knew how it was. They were irrepressible.

Shortly after my appointment I become a member of the Council of the Secondary Heads Association (my union, in effect), representing the independent sector, and I began to discover how free I had been, and still was, as a headteacher, by comparison with my peers in the maintained sector. They could not think and work creatively in the ways that I could because of the introduction of the National Curriculum and a multitude of national 'improvement' strategies.

When the DfES announced its new Key Stage 3 strategy, I went on behalf of SHA with other colleagues to meet representatives from the DfES. I wanted to explain that I, like others, had direct experience of transition from primary to secondary. We had all the pupils in our schools. I had been able to ensure seamless transition — from one side of the playground to the other. Teachers from my primary and secondary worked together; they observed one another's teaching. Some of them taught in both parts of the school although administratively they were separate schools. There were big sisters who went into little sisters' classes to help with reading, with art, with anything at all. I could ensure that the best teachers were working at all levels in the school — I never needed to direct the 'best' to GCSE or Advanced level classes. In fact, I knew that some of the best was taking place in Reception, and sometimes took myself off to Reception and other classes to see a supremely good focus on holistic learning.

All this, and there was still bafflement when pupils transferred from primary to secondary; they seemed to stop making progress — in fact, some of them seemed to regress: the symptom that the DfES was trying to address through the Key Stage 3 strategy. I thought I had good clues as to the causes and tried to persuade civil servants to listen; but I was, after all, from the independent sector; our information was plainly not going to be investigated. The DfES had its own thesis to prove.

I could watch it at first hand. Eleven-year-old girls who could take assembly for 300 without batting an eyelid, including issuing a dressing-down if needed; girls who sat with their own headteacher and told her what was needed by way of reform;

who behaved with sublime self-possession in a host of challenging situations, suddenly found that, by crossing the playground, they had been cast as little girls again.

Not only was this the allotted role, but the organizational principle seemed designed to reinforce their sense of helplessness and confusion. In essence, they spent the first year of secondary school learning how to manage themselves in a fast-changing and indirectly hostile environment, even though surrounded by friends and helpers. They had to adjust to a host of different adults; they were reminded at every turn that their grasp of knowledge was only tenuous because no sooner had they begun to assimilate it than a bell sounded and they were off again, on the pilgrims' way to another completely different person with completely different ideas and information to impart and no time at all to make sense of what they had just discovered.

I started to find out about emotional intelligence; about ways of working *with* aptitude and experience instead of *subverting* it.

No one developing the Key Stage 3 strategy seemed interested in finding out what many headteachers in the independent sector knew about all-age education and how to minimise the adverse effects of transferring from one phase to another.

I became increasingly irritated with the talk about *improving schools*. I had looked back at the records of Wimbledon High School. Yes, the public examination results had improved considerably over the previous 25 years — but this could be attributed to ever more refined and careful ways of preparing pupils for examination. I felt that the school which had produced Oxbridge professors who were happy to stay in touch with their former school had been excellent in its way. It had continued to be excellent because it had recruited staff who responded to and sustained its liberal ethos. But I was not convinced it was essentially 'better' now than twenty years ago, except in one regard: we were better at promoting diversity of talent — we were more effectively inclusive, in spite of the selective nature of the school.

Improving schools, in short, are schools which respond to what any particular group of pupils needs and wants; rather than schools which conform to a specific set of criteria.

In this school, pupils and staff implicitly taught newcomers how they needed to behave to belong, through their own models of behaviour. I often found myself meeting my three predecessors as head; we would all agree on the prevailing characteristics of the pupils; they had great generosity of spirit. As far as I am aware, the same is true now. Pupils would say to me, 'There's freedom of religion here.'

At WHS, again, I was able to work with highly vocal and challenging governors, led by Angela Rumbold, but her predecessor, former headteacher at a local comprehensive, was never far away. Another of the former heads had spent her life in the maintained sector before coming to WHS as headteacher. There was a high degree of awareness of what factors operate in the maintained sector.

Together we worked out what were the characteristics of a highly successful school, and whilst we did not formalize them into a code, we well understood what was crucial.

Ethos and the physical layout of the school were interlocked. The school has a focus which is easy to locate.

The assembly hall was at the heart of the school, with the head's study off one side, the staff room off another and classrooms too. It was like a market-place, identifiable as the centre. At any time of day you could see small groups of pupils and staff, talking, sitting, putting up posters, practising. You could lean over the balcony at the upper level and be a spectator.

Assembly took place here nearly every day; we did not want to enlarge the school to the point where we could not squash everybody in. Being together in the same place was powerful. It was confirmed for me here that the spirituality in a school supports not just its moral purpose but also its entire ethos.

At WHS, a non-denominational school, with plenty of Muslims, Hindus, some Jews, practising Christians of various denominations and conscientious agnostics too, the staff took assemblies and religious education very seriously. Hours were spent each term on planning so that all kinds of spirituality were acknowledged and encouraged. Every Year 7 class took part in a Passover Seder, let by a rabbi. In Year 9, every class enacted the Christian marriage service (much initial hilarity on the part of the bridegroom, father and best man, but girls soon adjusted to their roles). By the time they reached Year 10, they could confidently play out roles in 'The Big Question', tackling complex issues of behaviour with each of them being, for instance, a young Muslim mother, a Jewish father, a Sikh son — all giving responses as if they were living their parts.

The vocabulary used by the staff entirely supported and structured this culture. New staff rapidly discovered the language that was habitual and learned to use it; and I vividly recall the sense of astonishment and quiet outrage when someone arrived on the staff who did not seem to recognize or value this culture. They set out to work round her until she left.

Much of the talk you could overhear if you leaned out into the hall was wholly educational. Staff talked to pupils by arrangement; pupils buttonholed staff or one another in passing; people swopped information or planned another enterprise or rehearsal; and all this activity could be observed by the visitors who were waiting for appointments. At the time we had no real waiting area, no attractive front entrance, few of the appurtenances to impress outsiders about the success of the school. Yet, time after time, visitors would tell me how they saw everyone behaving with a tremendous sense of purpose.

Subject leaders would come to eat their sandwiches with me at lunch-times, just to talk education. I discovered that teachers were willing to work innovatively together in ways most managers would fear to suggest. They took possession of their work. A response to a request from me might be, 'Why do you want me to do that? Tell me what you want to achieve and I'll think of a better way of doing it.' I agreed, of course.

Given this degree of dialogue, we could organize our curriculum to match our educational principles. We asked all pupils to take Design and Technology for GCSE because we knew that some of our most academic pupils would find it hard and we wanted them to struggle, so that they would learn at school how to manage their own sense of imminent failure. Then the real learning might begin. They always achieved top grades (with much grumbling on the part of a few.)

We introduced a wide-ranging selection process to reveal the multiple intelligences in the candidates — including three- and four-year olds. One of my university professors had told me the department knew it could exchange fifty per cent of the students it had accepted with any other cohort of fifty per cent of those rejected, and the results would be the same. I looked at the Advanced level results of pupils who had been 'selected' at five and were still there at eighteen, by comparison with those who could have been said to be more rigorously chosen at the age of eleven. If anything, those who had been there the longest did better. School culture was more influential than apparent aptitude.

I never took for granted an excess of demand for places. I thought we needed to know how each child was talented in case there were fewer to choose from: bearing in mind 'no child can be allowed to fail'. I was wholly persuaded of the importance of making every child feel chosen, because of the emotional confidence it would give to both child and parents.

This influenced how we ran Special Educational Needs (SEN), not just for those perceived to struggle, but wherever there was a discrepancy between levels of aptitude. Every child could be special; certainly, every child was screened regularly, from Year 2 until Year 7 and thereafter if we judged it necessary.

We created a database full of information. We set about using this to make sure we could be analytical about what pupils were best at, so that we could encourage them to be more ambitious. We found study skills teachers who chose their work through personal experience and were intent on working with obviously able pupils who struggled, as well as those with specific learning difficulties. We developed 'case conferences', both of the high-level multi-agency type, and the informal sort where a tutor could call together everyone teaching a pupil for a brief meeting at coffee time. Specific concerns could be aired and tested, and more developed action could be planned if people were anxious. Staff began to take seriously their role as tutors and mentors, as well as subject teachers.

We introduced Thinking Skills throughout the school, starting from Year 2 and using different approaches. Almost all the programmes had the same intention: to stimulate questions and hypotheses rather than answers. I could actually track the difference between pupils with high cognitive ability but poor application of thinking, and those who applied their knowledge — who thought clearly.

This focus on special needs and multiple intelligences led me straight towards finding out as much as I could about how the brain grows, develops and learns. Everything I discovered confirmed that the brain is enormously plastic and malleable, in children. It is impossible to overstate the influence of parents and immediate experience on whether or not a child is 'bright' or perceived to be. Talk about 'bright working class children' could not be more ill-informed. The issue is of deprivation, not class; neglect, abuse and ignorance, not genetics. While at WHS, I discovered that we create intelligence to fit a post code, rather than developing intelligence regardless of birthplace — or birth.

Baroness Susan Greenfield, neuroscientist, was the godmother of a school pupil at Wimbledon, and visited the school to talk to pupils and parents. She showed us brain scans: one of the brain at work, learning a computer game, lit up by electrical activity. Another, however, showed the darkened brain successfully playing the computer game after learning it. A girl asked, 'For the brain to be all lit up does it have to be working? Does the brain have to be working for us to be learning?' She suddenly grasped that the brain alive and at work is actively forging connections between brain cells. So the measure of learning would not be 'success', at all. Brains that have succeeded in learning are quietly resting; brains that learn are active. To assess learning, we have to assess activity; at most, written examinations are recreated activity. Students who are not comfortable in 'recreating activity' and who fail the written examinations may still be highly competent learners.

At the same time I read about emotional intelligence, which

turned out to be as much a function of the brain as cognitive ability. This was another way of interpreting why pupils struggle to learn effectively when they move from one school to another: it is parallel to what happens when you move house — you may really want to do it and enjoy it, but huge amounts of emotional energy are consumed in dealing with the change itself and learning from the experience. Other kinds of learning are less likely to be important at such a time.

The importance of the focus on emotional intelligence in school life became particularly clear when we had to deal with tragedy.

One hot summer night at the end of term, after an end-of-year play performance, a group of Year 10 girls larked about on what they thought was a dead railway line. But the line was live and one of girls was electrocuted. They had to watch her die. The repercussions were felt throughout not just the year group but their parents, and the rest of the school too. I had not realized how close were the ties between pupils of different ages. I spent the rest of the summer holidays planning how to enable them to come back into school to complete their final GCSE year. We told the staff to stop worrying about GCSE results: the priority was to allow grief to take its course openly, naturally and with dignity. Of course we arranged for counsellors, but for the staff more than for the pupils, because pupils wanted first and foremost to talk to the teachers they knew and trusted. The adults needed support in managing the stress of listening to so much grief, guilt and loss. This year group had wonderful GCSE results because we tried to manage their emotional turmoil and stopped agitating about examination results and league tables. They had profound respect for this.

I could understand more clearly, then, how pupils as leaders actually affect the ethos of learning in a school. If they are emotionally engaged with their teachers in the learning — if teachers see themselves as facilitating the growing-up of young people into mature adults — then the entire culture is different. Pupils know how to be responsible for learning just as much as teachers, although in a different role. Curiously, in schools where the learning culture is so strong, teachers are much happier to be seen as learners too. One symptom is the willingness of staff to participate alongside pupils in performances — in choirs or orchestras, on stage or in sporting fixtures.

No one can be prescriptive about school culture. Each school has to find its own emotional framework and culture of belonging.

WHS had developed a drama tradition, started by the head of Drama, which enabled any members of Year 12 to form themselves into production companies and to spend up to six months working with an entire class in Year 7 and Year 8, to put on plays or musicals. It was extraordinarily powerful in the school culture. I just made sure that all Year 7 and Year 8 tutors were involved in supporting the rehearsal schedule rather than just the hapless head of Drama.

We trained Year 12 pupils, giving them elementary counselling skills so that they would know how to identify and manage behaviour, as well as how to understand the boundaries of confidentiality. They picked up so much information about young pupils and were so influential that they devoured the training.

The student leadership was created by staff and pupils together nominating and electing a team of about a dozen senior pupils, representing different areas of school life. This included a representative who acted as key link for each year group. The group was then left to elect the head girl. The roles of these pupils were not disciplinary at all — they bore no resemblance to conventional school prefects. They were indispensable in the leadership and management of pupils: they counselled the staff, organized events, took initiatives, led the School Council. Successive head girls were increasingly astute. They had better insight into leadership and management issues than many of the staff. I knew things were working correctly when, one after another, they politely told me how I could have managed something better, and what I should have done. Fine, I thought.

In November 1998, following an appraisal, I spent a week at The Grubb Institute, in a developmental programme called

'Leadership and Authority in Systems.' It changed my life. My appraiser knew that it would be powerful because she had followed the same course. I found myself looking at everything I was doing with fresh eyes. Perhaps the simplest way of expressing it was that I began to *hear* what my three daughters had been saying to me for years, instead of merely noting their comment. 'You ought to be doing this in the maintained system,' they kept saying. I remembered why I had entered teaching in the first place. My youngest daughter was now well on her way through university. I need no longer be driven by the wage-earner's imperative to keep the family going. I could do something for myself.

During that week I had begun to discover how important one's subconscious motives and processes are in directing one's actions. In both these independent schools I had primarily been driven by a desire for social justice: by a wish to see every child truly alive and excited. Many teachers feel the same. I realized that in my heart I wanted to work with the disenfranchized. For years I had been thinking of becoming a prison visitor; I was haunted by the image of someone 'locked up' — whether in a physical or psychological gaol. I told Angela Rumbold that I needed to finish my career in public service.

My background in Brighton

Brighton attracted me because it was my holiday home: I loved the sense of escape when I drove from London straight towards the sea at weekends, particularly at that moment when, about ten miles inland, you see the South Downs rising up before you. I associated them with the Bloomsbury set. As for Brighton itself, it was intensely pleasurable to wander past the crescents by the sea-front, and along the beach, to see people strolling and at ease. I loved it.

I knew a little about the Whitehawk estate and its reputation. Friends in Brighton would tell me about it. I went to Mass at St John the Baptist church in Kemptown and observed the oddly assorted population drawn from homes both squalid and beautiful — one of the joys, in fact, being the totally inclusive nature of such congregations. Anyway, I had read *Brighton Rock*, by Graham Greene. I knew about Pinkie and the race-course. My daughters always enjoyed prowling through The Lanes, and pre-West End productions came regularly to the Theatre Royal.

It was London-by-the-Sea: you could celebrity-spot if you wanted to. I knew nothing at all about the city's educational life, except its independent schools, three of which were very nearby. I also assumed that with two universities it must be a highly civilized place. It must have its black spots; all I saw were the homeless sprawled across benches or begging beside bank cash points.

When I was offered the post at East Brighton College of Media Arts, Angela Rumbold said that she wanted to stay in touch. She was deeply and genuinely interested — and hence instrumental in what I planned to do in Brighton once I understood what was required. I now set out to apply what I had learned and believed in the starkest of settings.

Chapter 3

Preparation

East Brighton College of Media Arts had started life as Stanley Deason High School, named for the visionary council member who established it, determined that the children of East Brighton should have a decent school. But after twenty years it had run into many problems. Its name was changed to Marina High School — in the hope, perhaps, that some of the affluence and buoyancy associated with the marina would attach itself to the school. I had been driving down to the marina for some time before I noticed Marina High School and thought what a lovely place for a school it must be. There was downland around it and seascape before it to lift the heart.

I saw the advertisement for the post of principal in the Fresh Start school, to open in 1999. Fresh Start schools have opened where schools have had a history of failure so endemic that the only possibilities seemed to be closure, or reopening as new legal entities: new staff, new names, new vision, and additional funding from the DfES. The funding amounts to about £1,000,000 of revenue over three years.

The funding is given to the Local Educational Authority (LEA) budget, for onward transmission into the school budget once the Raising Attainment Plan has been approved. The school must produce this plan; the LEA must create another, showing how it will support the school's intentions.

For Marina High School, this was a last attempt to redeem the school from what seemed to be inescapable failure. Six months later, the newly appointed principal had left and the school was back in Special Measures, having scarcely been out of them for several years. It was at this point that I applied for the post. I thought that since the circumstances were so extraordinarily desperate there might be a chance for me.

There had been seven headteachers in the previous ten years and I was to be the eighth. The record of the school was deeply dispiriting. About a fifth of the students officially on roll rarely attended. GCSE results placed it in the bottom 40 schools in the country. It was reviled in the press, I heard. Its name was ingloriously shortened to Comart — like a supermarket, everyone said.

I was prepared for unbelief about my appointment, but not for interest. Press reactions were overwhelming. For day after day at Wimbledon, once the announcement had been made, I seemed to have to set my work aside to talk to the press. The first wave was succeeded by another set of enquiries about my willingness to be part of a documentary. 'Can we be a fly-on-the-wall for six months in the new school?' There must have been at least six serious approaches by film and documentary makers.

But I had no intention of introducing cameras into so fragile a school. Cameras cause people to be aware of audience as if they were performers. The brain never forgets what is outside, even if the conscious mind does. This school community had already been too visible to an unsympathetic outside world. We needed to concentrate.

From July to December 2000

There were five key areas which had to improve before the school could be brought out of Special Measures; or inspectors would have to be convinced that the school was doing everything possible to improve. Staff and governors together with LEA advisers had created a forty-page Action Plan: ambitious, worthy, but somehow missing the point. The areas of failure were so significant that something radical would have to happen to transform the school.

I started working at once on what I would do, talking long and hard to Kathy Stonier, vice principal, and to Derek Bown, chair of governors. His backing and judgement were essential. He had spent years as a teacher and then an inspector of schools and there was little he did not understand about effective schools. Kathy had worked in difficult schools for years, with great success. We became not just colleagues, but friends.

I wanted to create a mental and emotional map for myself: to see how the school stood in relation to its community.

1. Drawing a line under the past

First and foremost, I did not look at the school's immediate past history.

I ignored the articles about the school published in *The Guardian* the preceding year; I did not want to know how my immediate predecessor had been appointed or had left, or how name changes had been arrived at, or what plans had been made for the Fresh Start. I knew people would tell me, soon enough. Before I had my imagination influenced by this intentional history, I wanted a mind that was uncluttered by other people's perceptions.

2. Investigation

Two of my Brighton friends had lived almost all their lives in the pleasant area of Woodingdean, on the downland at the top of the race-course. Jill had been a district nurse in East Brighton for much of her career. She knew the people well; but instead of trying to give me the history, she wisely sent me to the local health centre to discover what was current.

2a The health professionals I was warmly welcomed by district nurses and health visitors. (The only doctor was a locum —

no one would stay for any length of time; these robust women were the backbone for the medical provision.) I explained what I was about to do and asked them for their insights and views about the estate. No one had ever asked them what they thought, they said, and they were eager to talk. I paraphrase:

It looks tidy enough; but behind the neat doors there can sometimes be almost nothing. There is poverty. They don't keep their appointments at the Health Centre because lots of them don't know how to use a calendar accurately, so we make a simplified one for them. Of course, the ones who come here aren't the ones you really want to see. It's the ones who don't come. It's OK; there are just a couple of streets with the hard families. They rule the roost. Drugs — but only in a couple of streets. You'll meet lots of nineteen-year-old stepfathers. It's a sexualized estate. The woman has to have a man on her arm. You'll see the forty-year-old woman with the nineteen-year-old partner. Lots of grandfathers at forty; there's lots of incest. Domestic violence.

I asked them if they had any input into health education at the school.

Well, we did once — years ago — but not now. Yes, we'd love to help.

I was used to working with health professionals in schools. In fact, I thought they were vital. Sometimes a GP would ask me to refer a situation to social services or appropriate agencies because I could more easily do so as a headteacher than they could. I had also learned the hard way to read the small print of social services documentation, if ever it was presented to me.

I had come to rely on the presence of a full-time nurse on the staff to deal with the innumerable mental health problems in the adolescent population. I had found it far more reliable as a route than having a school counsellor. Anyone going to a counsellor would be signalling to everyone else in the community that she 'had a problem'. This acted as a powerful deterrent to many. Anyone going to a nurse could just be asking for aspirin; the direction of the conversation after that was no one else's business.

Getting a full-time nurse for the school (if possible with a background in mental health) would be a priority. The conversation with Whitehawk Health Centre staff had already outlined not just problems about sexual health but far more fundamental issues. The most alarming concerned language itself: the language addressed to young children.

'They use sexual language all the time to the children.' This was the background to its being 'a sexualized estate.' 'When the baby is very small it'll be a term of endearment — "you're a little cunt, aren't you?" And then when the baby's a couple of years old and getting difficult, it'll be "you fucking cunt".' I tried to imagine what the child would feel like; and these were the mothers who actually brought their children to the Health Centre where the staff listened to what was said. What was it like for the children whose mothers did not bring them? I extrapolated, and pondered.

2b The parish priest I had been a weekend and holiday member of the congregation of St John the Baptist church in Kemptown and construed that some of the others in the congregation would be College of Media Arts families. I introduced myself to the priest as the headteacher-to-be. 'Oh, it's you, is it?'

I said I wanted to pick his brains.

Yes, where possible families tried to send their children to Cardinal Newman School, the Roman Catholic secondary school in Hove. In fact, lots of children were presented for baptism just so that they could go to Cardinal Newman. No, the estate was nothing like as dangerous as it was said to be. One of the nuns still walked around perfectly happily late at night. She must be getting on for eighty now. Yes, he would love to help. Yes, he would gladly come into the school. No, he had never been asked.

I pondered again. I was used to religious leaders of different persuasions being part of school communities — sometimes through the formal process of assemblies, sometimes because they talked to faith groups in the school. I did not want to promote a particular kind of faith any more than a particular sort of intelligence or skill. I did, however, want pupils to think of faith as positive, real, enriching, just as intelligence was varied, vital for society, capable of growth, and equally valuable in all its forms.

All the schools with which I had been associated over the years had taken faith seriously. I wondered what I would find at the College of Media Arts.

3. The network

Although I did not want the media in the school at the outset, I thought they might be useful in the future; so I retained contact with everyone who had approached me. In addition, I started thinking about who else could be helpful. A Wimbledon parent was a song-writer who had written hits for Tom Jones, Engelbert Humperdinck and others. He had taught Wimbledon girls to write pop songs. He was the sort of Londoner who would be convincing, I suspected, for adolescent boys. I asked if he would be prepared to visit. Yes. I met Glenda Jackson at a workshop. Yes, she would come. Rosie Millard, the BBC Arts Correspondent, was a former pupil at Wimbledon. Yes, I could write to her.

I worked my way through a list, just asking. I did not think anything would be immediate, but I knew that I passionately wanted a radio station for the school. Any contacts could be helpful. For instance, I would want to approach Fat Boy Slim.

Other parts of the network were very different. I could not afford to overlook the school's poor reputation with the teacher unions and arranged to meet Steve Sinnott, who was the Deputy General Secretary of the National Union of Teachers (NUT). I talked to him about how I had worked with teacher unions in other schools; to show that I would work *with* not against unions. I was an active union member myself.

The Director of Education in Merton explained how she was developing a multi-agency approach, and shared with me the development plan for the borough, which drew together different strands. She wanted me to understand, too, some of the political duplicity that operates in local education authorities. She was herself a victim — having experienced a successful Ofsted inspection, she was being ousted.

The Director of Schools Personnel at Brighton rang with a problem about the pay for teaching assistants and wanted to know what I thought. Together we worked out a strategy for a promotion ladder for teaching assistants, with the highest levels of pay we could devise within the constraints. He had a dry Northern humour that appealed to me. My network already included some of my future colleagues.

4. Analysis

I began to think about the whole framework of teaching and learning. Derek Bown and Kathy Stonier had described the totally unplanned curriculum for media arts when the school was redesignated a Fresh Start school. They related that the then Director of Education, her advisers and the Education Committee of the Council had no coherent concept of media arts and its curricular implications. The staffing difficulties had been enormous, nor were there appropriate facilities until the summer of 2003, by which time the decision finally to close the school was taken. Even the computer network, though large, had been hopelessly inefficient because the need for high-level technical support had not been recognized. However, the acting principal had appointed a good manager for the system, so I could make some assumptions about the future of information and communication technologies (ICT) in the school.

The acting principal had been seconded from the Education Action Zone (EAZ) to run the school for six months until I could take up the post. EAZs were another way in which the DfES tried to help schools where pupils did not reach acceptable standards of education. Schools were required to work together, following a joint action plan, using additional funding which was provided jointly by the DfES and business partners from within the area of the Zone. In some EAZs, the action plans were drawn up by the local headteachers who also decided how the money was to be spent. In others — and this was one of them — the Director of the EAZ made the decisions, and most funding was used to appoint consultants who would supplement the work of the LEA advisers.

I had a very clear idea about what Media Arts should be, and reliable ICT was essential. I was used to operating in an increasingly sophisticated and very well-resourced environment within GDST, constructed on the premise that online and distance learning would soon be commonplace; that the teacher would stand alongside the pupil, rather than being above, as the fount of all knowledge.

The new technology should be used to release creativity, not in humdrum ways; and students needed to think about the moral and ethical choices that would inevitably come their way, made more complex by the new possibilities.

The name 'East Brighton College of Media Arts' was cumbersome and a nuisance; but the concept of teaching through media was powerful — not least because I was certain the students would be far more confident than the staff. This was critical, because if the levels of literacy were as low as was rumoured, then I needed to know what the students' positive skills were. These would be the starting point. You need experience of excellence before you can understand what someone is asking you to aim for — especially if you think that you are stupid. Students were likely to be better than their teachers at managing the technology.

5. Senior members of staff: planning how to work together

It proved curiously hard in my early meetings with the senior staff to elicit any kind of information. 'How do you normally handle this?' I asked them about some routine matter. 'But what will *you* want?' was the baffling response.

'You're the eighth head in ten years,' they reminded me. Some of these predecessors had been 'standing in' for two or three months; some had stayed for two or three terms or two or three years. It was all the same: no one had stayed long enough to build the long-term relationships which are essential if behaviour, attitudes and expectations are to change. I had already found out that it takes about four years in post for the head to feel s/he can clearly identify the differences his/her presence has made in a school.

Whatever their skills, the senior staff had been unable to use them to full effect because there had been no one taking the full role of headteacher. In those early conversations I began to understand what is meant by leadership — even though I had been practising it, had written about it, given seminars about it.

Leadership takes many forms, but one is like being the keystone in the arch. You have to feel your relationship to all the others. Their actions and presence exert pressure on you. You have to retain your shape — your role. You must not be distracted from this.

There are lists of competencies and qualities and skills galore; these include the National Standards for Headship. But what I experienced throughout my previous headships was that the head has to 'feel the school on the pulses' — to paraphrase what Keats had to say about poetry.

You need to sense everything that is happening; to cross-reference almost everything you are told, so that you are not vulnerable to hearsay; to analyse with rigour; and to be bold.

When these experienced teachers said, 'Yes, but what will you want?' I saw that I needed to help them remember that they had authority. The way in which leaders behave defines the ways in which everyone belongs, and the decisions they take. It isn't 'what I do,' but 'what we do'. It is as if you draw a map on the floor and say, 'There it is, there's our territory. We do it like this.' What we planned together enabled us to focus on what was essential to put things right: relationships and behaviour, the nature of the curriculum, who would take responsibility for what, and on what basis.

5a. Planning for relationships and behaviour The student behaviour was at the forefront of most people's thoughts. It was what everyone had told me about; the issue that probably worried me most and least. I couldn't wait to meet them; but I feared that they would not take to me because I might seem so alien.

'Tell me what is likely to happen,' I said. 'Well, they'll tell you to fuck off and then they'll run away.' I imagined it for a moment. I didn't think I would cope very well with being told to 'fuck off' by someone who then disappeared; and then I thought, well, if I can't cope with it, why should anyone else do so?

Plainly, this was not the worst that could happen. There could be running fights or actively deranged behaviour, but what most affects teachers is the attrition of feeling alone and helpless in the face of adolescent defiance. Whether it is violent or mute, this defiance means, 'You have nothing to say that remotely interests me. I don't have to pay attention to you. You have nothing for me.'

I had to start with what I as principal felt confident about.

Day to day talk and interaction sets the tone; students should be able to rely on the behaviour of adults as calm, consistent, just and firm. No adult should talk offensively to a student; and if students are offensive and unsafe in their behaviour, they should be put outside the boundary for a while to cool off. This should give them time to recover or learn self-discipline, if only at a very basic level. Then they can be congratulated. At a simple level, the rule of thumb for adults is: don't shout. Don't order about. Don't talk to a group of adolescents in a way that would offend you if you were part of that group.

I would not expect staff to be made to feel uncertain because students were running off. Making the school feel safe was one of the first priorities.

5b. Planning the approach to discipline Together we drew up a protocol: a way of drawing that boundary around the school to say, 'You may behave like this out of school, and we will pass no judgement on that. But in school, we all behave like this.' We agreed that being clear about this boundary for behaviour would help everyone.

If a student swore and then ran, s/he would be excluded for two or three days. There would be an interview with parents before s/he could come back to school, and a contract that would define not just what we expected of student and parents, but what the school staff would do to support the student. We would be able to reward improved behaviour.

I asked for a list of the students who were most likely to be aggressively disruptive. If we already knew who they were, we ought to be able to devise a strategy for managing each one before the incident erupted. There were fifty-five students on the list: ten percent of the students on roll. I had always worked on the assumption that if a student was difficult there was a good reason for it. The scale on which this exercise had to be developed suggested how complex the process was likely to be. We would have to be creative.

Instead of letting one member of the leadership team bear the brunt of the discipline, we would promote a new model to all the staff and students : discipline was collective, not individual. The work of any one member of staff would be supported by everyone else, and no one person would ever be expected to take sole responsibility. This principle would work in classrooms, too. If a teacher had discipline problems with a group, we would all assume that the teacher was doing a professional job but was in need of assistance, and that we would investigate, analyse and support.

I wanted to make sure that the women in the leadership team were allowed to take the lead in maintaining discipline, instead of deferring to a stereotype.

5c. Planning the curriculum I knew the curriculum was at the heart of the problem. When I was bored as a schoolgirl I had plenty of opportunities for diverting myself — some of them invisible to my teachers, and some causing them inconvenience; but on the whole I complied. Most children with good life-chances comply.

When teachers are engaged in extra-curricular work with students, they almost invariably find that students are enthusiastic and willing to put up with serious discomfort and boredom because they choose their involvement. It is one of the most rewarding experiences you can have as a teacher. Teachers need to be creative again — to draw on professional experience and skill, to develop new approaches to the curriculum, to give it the responsive, personal characteristics of chosen extra-curricular learning.

We devised 'the dynamic culture', with four key areas, each of which would be the responsibility of the four assistant principals. They would have new roles rather than a series of tasks. This would help them to know the extent of their authority — their right to take initiatives without having to check with me first. I wanted them to feel in charge and to respond to students quickly. These students needed things to happen now, not in some indeterminate future.

I wanted students to experience something excellent, so that they had a sense of what *excellence* felt like. I wanted them to learn constructively, so that they had a sense of what *intentional learning* felt like: learning that was planned, rather than accidental; positive rather than damaging. I wanted them to enjoy learning — any sort of learning would do — so that they had faith in their own capacity to learn in the future.

Recurring problem: small fires on the downland, usually lit by young boys from the school. I had to toe the party line about this and understand the concerns shared by both the caretaker and the Fire Service. But in my heart I thought about learning to light fires myself — first as a reluctant Girl Guide and then as an adult making camp-fires. My own children learned to cook dampers and bacon; we had camped beside a Scottish loch, climbed mountains, jumped into mountain streams and tarns, constructed castles from cardboard to bring Narnia to life... I had a strong memory from early childhood of a bottle of magic water and spells; a vivid street life interwoven with books.

The best teachers at the College of Media Arts were gloriously ingenious. In one of Helen's first lessons at Marina High School, she placed a worksheet on each desk, only to discover the entire class solemnly eating them. Her response for the next lesson with this class was to sellotape the worksheets to the desks. When teaching *Macbeth* to the bottom set for Key Stage 3 English, Helen, wonderful teacher but not an English specialist, created puppet theatres with her class. The students were entranced and wholly willing to animate the characters to make the plot unfold.

Everyone in the leadership team had an ethical drive to change the life circumstances of students who not only came from difficult backgrounds but were effectively pilloried for doing so.

It is essential to have this commitment from a strong team of adults at the heart of a school like the College of Media Arts — and they should all be generously paid, too. They put their personal lives to one side for a while, because such schools take all of one's professional resource and much of what is personal, too. We spent long hours together at both ends of the school day. Families and friends have to live with absence, either physical or emotional or both.

The victim mentality

In one of those meetings at the end of 2000, I heard stories of the bevy of inspectors and advisers who seemed to be pressing their action plans on the school. I had no idea of the insidious power of the 'done to' culture, because I had never been part of one before. This is how it was presented to me — ***Done to:***

- By the LEA (all villains, of course, ready to stab you in the back — 'watch your back, Jill' — an off-stage villain plotting downfall and ruin, but never actually identifiable on stage as a specific individual with evil intent).
- By Her Majesty's Inspectors of Schools (HMI: not so villainous, because not the LEA, but wicked even so, for not appreciating how hard it was to work at this school and how heroic people were who endured there).
- By the Department of Education and Skills, especially the Fresh Start unit, delegates from which had apparently declared that the staff were all responsible for the school's plunge back into Special Measures (in this case, individuals from the unit were clearly labelled as insensitive).

- By the other schools in Brighton and Hove, all terrified of having College of Media Arts students in their intake, possessed of considerable skill in divesting themselves of anyone who 'ought really to be at College of Media Arts', and sending them in the direction of the latter (this being very clever and devious because parents could *request* a place at the College of Media Arts when they were being encouraged to remove their child from another school — before said child was excluded — so that the Admissions office could exert that other lever, 'parental preference').

- By the dinner party circuit of Brighton, fuelled by media speculation, which thrilled to the gossip about atrocious behaviour in the school and on the estate, and which cited a series of articles written by Nick Davies, which appeared in *The Guardian* during 2000, and which drew attention to the difference between East Brighton College of Media Arts (at the time called Marina High School) and Roedean barely a mile away.

My team seemed to take it for granted, but I was indignant. 'No one is going to tell *us* what to do. We have all the necessary skills here.' One of them impressed on me the importance of saying the same to the staff when I met them all for the first time. I knew from independent schools that no one from outside can do anything, really, except advise, withdraw a budget or close a school. Only those on the inside make the difference.

Partnerships

After all this planning I wanted to find the other key partners I would be working with, so that I could start to plan with them too. Working with governors was easy; I was in constant communication with Derek Bown as chairman and followed his guidance. He was an insider. The other key partners were outside: the LEA and the parents.

Parents

I had met some parents in November 2000, when I went to the Annual General Meeting of governors and parents. Unbelief was quite clear. 'You say you'll do things,' they said, 'but how do we know you will?'

I did not attempt to justify myself by explaining what I had done through two previous headships. At the Royal Naval School, I had invited parents to shadow their daughters for a day. There was a protocol of understanding for this — they had to attend every lesson (no picking and choosing); I would not change any teacher as a result.

At Wimbledon, we had made an announcement each week in the bulletin that went home, announcing that any parent could come to see me without appointment and without saying why, during a specific hour each week. This worked really well, although it had begun life as a poor relation of the 'shadowing for parents' experience offered at the Royal Naval School. At Wimbledon High there was no room in some of the crowded classrooms for a single other body, so no shadowing was possible, but the weekly appointments were always taken up by a few parents. I would deal with whatever they raised. Sometimes they just came for a chat. Twice a term I set aside a morning to talk to groups of parents. I had loved this.

All I could say to the unbelieving parents of the College of Media Arts was that I would ring them as soon as I started working January 2001 and arrange to meet them. 'I have to make a promise and you have to see me keeping it,' I said. 'I will have to keep on doing this. Then gradually you will know how to believe me.'

I introduced a weekly bulletin for parents. It was easy to read, with a friendly font and lots of clipart images to enliven its appearance. It was a start, even though staff complained about the litter of paper darts; students were not used to friendly communications from school to home. More to the point, most of them did not possess school bags; that was a different sort of battle. Each week in the bulletin there was an announcement that parents could come to see me without having to say what they wanted to discuss.

I suppose that in the two years I was there perhaps only a couple of dozen parents took the opportunity. I had to find other ways of reaching them.

Local Education Authority (LEA)

I talked to the Assistant Director for School Improvement often enough to trust her ideas and judgements. She was to be my main contact as a Council Officer; but in December 2000, I went to a meeting with most of the education officers to establish what I would do. Could I quickly work on a new Action Plan; on an Education Plan?

One key area for discussion during the whole process of my being appointed was the number of students on roll. To me, this was all too familiar territory since it occupied a great deal of energy in the independent sector. I suggested that it would probably take about five years for the school roll to rise from its current number (about 500) to a desired number of 700. Everyone seemed to agree that this was realistic; but I knew how hard it would be to achieve. I asked the assembled officials what would happen if I made the school educationally sound, but the roll did not rise. There was some shifting in seats, and then, 'But that won't happen, really it won't.' I did not attempt to argue. I knew that it all too easily could, but there was no point in contesting it at this stage. In any case, I thought that the LEA itself could make a huge difference. It would not be like operating in a totally free and market-driven culture, as I had been used to in the independent sector. This was one of the major reasons for my changing from independent to maintained schools: I wanted to make sure that students could get what they really needed and deserved, rather than having to play the market.

In all my thinking and preparation I had assumed that I had been appointed because of my previous experience and whatever qualities the governors perceived me to have, and that I would be able to make whatever decisions were needed to make the school educationally sound. This proved not to be the case.

The Fresh Start at East Brighton College of Media Arts had been not impressive. The idea of 'media arts' had been suggested to the Council by a local businessman who thought the new media industries in Brighton could work alongside a school. The Council seized upon the idea of a school, but did not place it in a context of vigorous local employment because, as noted earlier, there was plainly no concept of what 'media arts' might be.

The new principal was the previous head of Marina High School. There was no provision for a Special Educational Needs Coordinator (SENCo) in the reopened school, despite the soaring numbers of students with high levels of need. Large numbers of new computers were bought and networked together; but there was no network manager with the skills and experience to lead and advise the staff. Half of the staff were reappointed from Marina High School: staff with long and bitter memories. The principal feared the recurrence of unionized activity in the staff-room, so he removed the staff-room as a meeting place. Staff had few ways of meeting or discovering how to work together. Within a few months almost all the staff appointed new to the school had resigned, and school culture reverted, depending on the loyalties and expertise of those who had been there for years. Essentially, no one was clear about the school's purpose, importance to the community or identity.

Stanley Deason: civic vision

The history of the school belied this gloomy outcome. Alderman Stanley Deason had set about tackling social injustice some 80 years previously. He had been very troubled about the dim life-chances of the children brought up on the Whitehawk estate. He knew about the scare stories in Brighton at large. The inhabitants of Brighton did not look kindly on Whitehawk, with myths being promulgated from the 1930s to the 1970s and beyond. Brighton residents frightened themselves with a fairy story about Whitehawk; but Stanley Deason resolved to change this.

Twice leader of the Labour group, he was an outspoken and principled politician, so respected that even when the Conservatives led Brighton Council he was invited to chair the education committee. In 1963, the Tories chose him to be Mayor of Brighton. He was one of the prime movers in the discussions about starting a university in Sussex, beginning in the 1950s — but it was the school for Whitehawk and Queen's Park which probably best embodied his passion for social justice. He felt strongly about giving the children of Whitehawk the opportunity they deserved.

Stanley Deason believed that he had achieved his aim when the school was officially opened in 1977, with the Lord Chancellor presiding at the opening ceremony. Simultaneously, Brighton Council ceased to be self-governing and the focus for decision-making moved to East Sussex. This was one of the key features in the disintegration of the school in Whitehawk. Brighton Council did not become self-regulating again until 1999.

Although they named the Leisure Centre for Stanley Deason, and a bus, too (as is the Brighton custom), hardly anyone remembers him. No one in the school I joined in 2001 spoke about Stanley Deason, although there were staff who must have known him. He died in 1983. His wife was a member of the governing body and left the school a legacy when she died. No one at the school recalls this. There was no trace in any of the documents I was handed. All the original idealism seemed to have vanished.

Chapter 4

Term 1: Spring 2001

I rehearsed the first meeting with staff many, many times so that I could find a voice inside myself which would be authentic. That first meeting would be critical. As headteacher you can issue whatever commands you think will impress — but you cannot be round the corner where the staff are alone with students. You have no option but to trust the strengths, the conscience and the motivation of your staff. You cannot motivate them; but you *can* create the conditions for people to find their motivation.

I told them that we did not need anyone from outside to tell us what to do; and that our relationships with the students were of prime importance. They seemed enormously relieved. I had asked them to put first what they were already good at.

After that, I needed to put my own relationship with students to the test. I took to the corridors.

It was exhilarating to find my touch. I loved talking to the boys. I had taught boys at Wimbledon — the articulate and argumentative members of the Sixth Form at Kings College, Wimbledon — but this was different. College of Media Arts boys were curious about me, teasing, testing my vocabulary. They wanted to sort out for themselves what I would do; but they were also comfortably impersonal. I was strongly reminded of a litter of puppies as they struggled crossly to get first into a dining room or through the door of a classroom. It was vital to convey calm, firmness, purpose in the way I stood and moved; I had to say what I meant in simple, unmistakable, respectful terms; to pitch my voice low. I wanted them to feel that when I was on the corridors, instilling order, I was delighted to be there. And I was — I never lost the pleasure of the corridor patrol.

Overwhelmingly the hardest part was not knowing the students by name in those early days. By naming, you draw them into relationship with you. From the outset, I insisted on being 'Dr Clough' rather than 'Miss.' This created further confusion. 'Do you have a surgery then?' 'I've got a stye in my eye,' and so forth. I had to explain. 'I call you by your name and I expect you to call me by mine.' It became for me one of the measures of change and improvement; if they could remember to call me by name, they were beginning to grasp something about how to relate. But it was hard not to be beguiled when, after a few days, I looked across a walkway into a class where, instead of working, they were watching me go by. Suddenly there were hands waving at me. I could see that they were calling out, 'Hello Miss.' The girls took to waving at me in passing: 'Hello Miss — Dr — Miss.'

In those early days I had to be all over the building (getting lost), just making basic straightforward decisions to establish for staff and students alike what sort of school this was going to be with me as its principal. I knew exactly what to do. It was a huge relief.

The building: why the Private Finance Initiative was planned (PFI)

Taking to the corridors gave me insight into one of the reasons for the school's problems: it was geographically dysfunctional, too. The building had been put up in three distinct phases, designed — if one can name it as such — as a series of boxes set into the downland, each at a different level, and only linked by stairs from the lowest levels. You could not access one upper level from another without trekking down flights of stairs, along corridors and then up other flights of stairs. Some of the corridors were open to the rain and wind. There was no centre to the school; no physical heart to which people could gravitate, and which could become the emotional heart of the school. On the contrary, the effect of these linked boxes was to make the school seem like a maze; you could turn and turn again, seeing through windows the place where you wanted to go, but not knowing which route to take. The symbolic effects of this were extraordinarily haunting.

I had already asked for the principal's study to be moved, before I arrived. From the opening of Stanley Deason High School, the head's study seemed to be as far away from students as possible, tucked away at the end of a series of rooms. To reach the head you had to pass any number of administrators. I knew that the head should be right at the heart of things: highly visible. Staff and students needed to know how to reach you without bureaucracy, because of the model for leadership the head must provide.

This desire for visibility brought me at once up against the projected PFI plan for four schools in Brighton. PFI is a government programme which allows private companies to build facilities such as schools and hospitals for public use. The private company retains ownership of the facilities, which are leased by the public organizations usually for 25 years, during which time the company can recoup its investment through the charges it makes for the use of the facilities. The contract allows the company to lease the buildings to agencies other than, for instance, the school, provided that this does not conflict with the school's requirements. The private companies are meant to take the risks that the public agencies would otherwise incur in developing new and expensive facilities.

In Brighton, as in many other authorities, the LEA decided to bid for a PFI contract because it could not afford to improve its schools without funding from external sources. Three well established schools were selected, two of which were highly sought after. East Brighton College of Media Arts had been added to the project, I was told, as a token of good faith on the part of the authority. The LEA wished the school to succeed, and to acquire facilities that the school could not provide for itself through attracting income in the form of funding per head, since its student roll had been falling for several years.

I was well aware of how complex the plans for new and rebuilding can be, from having lived through the process in both my previous schools. Moving the principal's study was not just a symbolic act, but one with precise financial and planning implications. It signalled the beginning of the long and puzzling negotiations for PFI. I was troubled by the discrepancy, between educational vision and principle and the bidding process for PFI. On the one hand, compromises must be reached, but on the other, educational principles ought not to be jeopardized: that was my experience as well as my belief — and at that early stage, before any contractor had been agreed, it was easy to decide to move the principal's study. The vice principal, Kathy Stonier, consulted the chair of governors and it was as simple as that because they both heartily agreed with why I wanted the change.

Alternative plans submitted by different PFI bidders were already in school, as were bulky documents full of complex information. I looked at them and looked away — nothing was going to distract me from concentrating on students and staff at this point, however inadequate the building.

The nature of the leadership

Effective schools develop over many years, with governors, staff and parents all understanding their roles. When you start out as a headteacher, you are able to take or reject the role that a particular school offers you. In my first headship, I found a culture where the staff all expected to shake hands formally with the head at the end of each term, as she ticked off their names on a list. Not my style or beliefs — and a strong indicator of how hard it would be to liberate the independent self inside each of the staff at that school. But it would have to be done, so that the pupils could become independent and responsible young women. My role as 'leader' in that school had a specific context: the cultural association of the school with the Royal Navy. What kind of leadership did one find in the armed forces? historically, and now? or in the City? Once I understood these, I could work out how to become the appropriate model for *leader* in that school.

At the College of Media Arts, few people had any sense of leadership because the school's history had demolished it. Those people who did understand were unable to take up their leadership roles to full effect unless the principal completed the pattern: being the keystone in the arch — making a bridge rather than a pile of assorted stones.

During that first term I spent an enormous amount of time asking questions. Whenever I embarked on a discussion with almost anyone who had been on the staff for more than a term, the same sorts of issues would surface. The feeling of being 'done to' could not just be swept aside as unreasonable. It had some serious truths concealed within it.

Virtually all the external agencies involved with the school assumed not only that their representative should advise school staff on how to improve, but also that staff would follow their instructions, because someone *from outside* knew better — in almost any sphere you can think of. The school failed because the staff were inadequate, incompetent or ignorant — this was the implication. Moreover, these agencies had budgets: they could make things happen, they thought, because they controlled budgets that the school could not. Therefore they could provide advice and exert pressure to make things happen in the ways they thought right because they had money to make their ideas work.

Whilst I listened to the talk about poor teaching, and went looking at lessons for myself, I mused on the fact that I had seen plenty of merely ordinary teaching in the independent sector — in schools that were much sought after. I had observed bored and occupied pupils, rather than pupils avidly learning — but that had not impaired their overall engagement because the schools could engender a strong sense of belonging. And there was always the freedom to find other ways of learning within the school's culture.

I remembered all this when the leadership team at the College of Media Arts asked me what duties I would undertake on the rota. This meant lunch duty, break duty, detention duty and so on.

In independent schools I had swept the hall floor at midnight to clear up broken glass; I had carried and arranged all the chairs in a sports hall one Sunday afternoon to prepare for speech day; I had climbed over a flat roof in pouring rain and darkness looking for a missing pupil; I had required students to put their chewing gum into the palm of my hand; and I had always taught whatever was most challenging in a school — all these as necessary for a headteacher. But I was disconcerted by a request to step forward as part of a lunch duty rota.

How the headteacher fills his/her time signals priorities to everyone else. I took the view that the prime role of a school is to develop experience and expertise in intentional learning. I always taught a central subject — that is, not filling in for teachers who were absent, but a subject that would be examined externally — because in this way I subjected my own teaching and interaction with students to the same criteria as the rest of the staff. If I was calling people to account for their standards of teaching, I would be called to account too. If there was some new and troubling examination system or method of assessment, I would be as involved as any newly qualified teacher. At a different level, by teaching a mainstream subject (English) I would have to operate the systems of my own school. Whatever the system for writing reports, or marking work, I would have to experience it.

At another level still, I would have the same opportunities as all other members of staff to hear from students at first hand what they thought about their school. It was the best feedback of all, because they were invariably honest. Adults might temper their language because they were talking to the employer; students rarely compromised.

In this school where everyone from outside pointed at poor standards of teaching and learning as being fundamental, you would have expected the new principal to spend most of her time behaving like an Ofsted inspector and observing lessons. The leadership team did want me to do this, of course; but duties loomed large.

When I was required to join break or lunch duty rotas, I wondered rather desperately who would be doing what I had always done: be available when staff and students were not in classes for them to walk through the door to say, 'I think you could have done that differently,' or 'I have an idea. What do you think about. . . ?' or 'I've been sent by my English teacher to show you my work.'

Who else was going to drop in at the lunchtime choir rehearsal — actually, hoping to participate? — or sit in the school office to see how the administrative staff coped with the usual onslaught?

I am certain that headteachers should be written into main school processes and systems; but that the system you choose sets the priority for achievement in the school. Long ago, a headteacher said to me, picking up crisp packets as we walked along a corridor, 'I could make this the best school in the country for Tiddly Winks. I choose not to do so.'

My concept of leadership had at its core the belief that I needed to spend a lot of time with students and staff so that I could demonstrate rather than explain what I thought leading and learning in a school should be. I thought behaviour was best managed by creating situations where students could initiate, could show their interest, enthusiasm or initiative; rather than reacting to situations in which students behaved badly and needed to be told off.

When it was assumed that I would participate in a rota without questioning the underlying symbolic value of my action, I thought to myself, 'I'm playing a bit part here. I don't mind — I've often played the bit part, but who will play the head's part?'

The problem of playing the bit part as well as being the director is that you are in danger of being diverted by detail from looking at the map as a whole. You need to position yourself so that you can switch perspective from part to whole, from minutiae to strategy — but it is dangerous to be trapped in one role alone.

Approach to leadership: discipline strategy

I discovered how to transform the bit part into part of my own role as soon as I took to the corridors. I was able to engage with students at their most intransigent. A small but significant number of students lived in the corridors because they rejected the classrooms. So meeting them on corridors gave me the chance to establish the vocabulary of conversations. I would ask, 'What do you most enjoy doing? What do you want to do when you leave school? What are you good at?' This usually provoked incomprehension, and was highly informative.

When someone said, 'I want to be a lorry driver,' I would say, 'That's great — but you need to know how to service the engine. You want to be able to run your own fleet of lorries. You need to be an engineer. You need some business skills.' They never disagreed, although I expect in their hearts they thought what I suggested was unrealizable.

I also seized the chance to reinforce key messages with staff. Staff were free to call for support from whoever was on patrol. You would be summoned to an area or a classroom by the walkie-talkie and then there were different scenarios: the problem — that is, the angry altercation — had vanished; or the member of staff had worked with someone in a neighbouring classroom to remove a particular student (stage two of the protocol); or the student was glaring angrily at the member of staff; or — worst case — the member of staff was angry, too.

For two terms I automatically took the student away to a Time Out room which we had established for the purpose. The Time Out room was staffed, too. Students could sit quietly and work; or talk over with the person on duty what had happened to cause upset. Each incident was logged, so that we could look for recurring patterns of behaviour. The intention was always the same: to let the teacher re-establish a calm and orderly classroom environment; to give the student time to recover too, and to reflect on what had happened.

I found, though, that the same students tended to be sent to the Time Out room; many went once or twice, found it was boring, thought it was better to stay in class. There were fewer difficult incidents. The persistent offenders, however, were those to whom normal, reasonable processes would not be likely to apply. It was also very expensive as a management process: one member of staff on patrol, another on containment — when what was needed was deeper analysis so that we could work towards prevention rather than cure.

As an interim arrangement it was highly successful. In the first half-term, I excluded a large number of students for short periods of time. Everyone else appreciated the firm stand; and even those who were sent home were, by and large, content to accept the discipline because the boundary was clear. As for the staff, they could see that nothing was inevitable. If students behaved badly, adults could analyse, understand, plan and carry out a course of action. We started to create the culture where poor behaviour could be seen as a symptom rather than as a cause.

We evaluated the use of the Time Out room and closed it after a couple of terms because we needed to move on: to find more purposeful ways of engaging students in classes, rather than removing them. I had a stronger grasp of what needed to happen next. If students have very narrow and tedious life-experiences, school needs to displace these by a host of rich and memorable ones. The Time Out room showed us how the curriculum needed to change, as well as teaching styles.

The other simple action I took after two terms of walking the school was to unlock the doors (apart from obvious exceptions: laboratories, technical areas to which only supervised access should be given). I was tired of acting as a kind of prison warder, segregating different parts of the school population in an attempt to control it. I decided to trust the students.

Developing new strategies: planning for success rather than reacting to failure

I knew that we needed to plan several simultaneous courses of action, some of them short-term and some that might be years in development. There could be no 'quick fixes' and I was not interested in anything that smacked of gimmick. No one should be spending time or resources on actions that were superficial. For instance, we decided not to follow the General National Vocational Qualification (GNVQ) in ICT that so many schools adopt. GNVQs are intended to appeal to students because of their more obvious preparation for employment than conventional GCSE examinations. This particular GNVQ gives students the equivalent of four GCSEs and so provides a swift gain in GCSE point scores and league tables. 'It's boring,' I was told. Too many of these students skipped lessons or school altogether because they were bored; but on the other hand we added Food Technology because we thought boys would love the chance of cooking. They did. It was a great pleasure to see, six months later, boys queuing up to make pizzas in class.

Among my parallel courses of action were:

- Try to get a school nurse at once.
- Investigate resources (including budgets) externally.
- Start collating information about a radio station.
- Recruit at least one primary school teacher.
- Put in place some decent systems for finding out what students could do — *positive* information as well as the depressing facts about their levels of literacy.
- Plan substantial and sophisticated training for staff for dealing with a very difficult population of students, rather than the condescending training which assumed that teachers were inadequate, and failed to recognize the highly developed interpersonal skills of many of them.

- Set up regular 'off timetable days', to provide a multitude of different learning experiences which students could *choose* and which would be *fun*. I urgently wanted them to discover that being at school could combine having fun and learning enthusiastically. Most of them would not choose extra-curricular activity; so this would have to become part of normal school.

Independent schools allocate many resources to the extra-curricular. I knew from experience that there was more than enough time in the curriculum to cover the defined materials — if students knew how to learn they would do so very fast — so I encouraged all sorts of informal learning, making sure that everyone had a chance to take part, not just the most difficult. There was a good deal of resentment at the fact that students at risk of exclusion seemed to have more outings than others.

Initially, there was anxiety about this: 'Yes, but what about the National Curriculum?' I really did not care. Everyone knew that I was right, because all teachers have the same experience of seeing students excited by something they choose to do (playing football in a school team; being on stage; planning a charity event); and — more important — seeing how well the students do it, too, and how readily they accept adult support and advice instead of resenting it.

One of my most grateful memories is of the HMI Monitoring Inspector who was prepared to see this in operation and to endorse its importance.

A visit coincided with a planned day on building personal and team skills, which took place in the Summer Term 2001. We thought long and hard about cancelling it in order to present conventional teaching but decided not to. It was a significant part of the strategy for getting out of Special Measures, linked with the Personal Development programme.

The second inspection day would be conventional, but for the first, two HMIs walked the school seeing staff interacting with students at their best: with excellent personal relationships, high levels of skill in managing groups of potentially crotchety students who did not really like each other, and trying out new ideas to inspire confidence and self-esteem in students.

It was a great day, giving HMI plenty of opportunities to observe students eager to learn, launching themselves with enthusiasm into unpredictable pursuits. It demonstrated that we were finding creative ways of transforming the school ethos, of finding measures for improvement.

I felt mightily encouraged at the end of it because, whilst bewailing their exhaustion, staff realized that we really could *obviously* help students to progress.

Some of the informal activities were simple and cheap (essential, given the levels of poverty at home). The Science department simply took younger students to the beach — every year, there were Year 7 students who had never been to the beach they could see from the estate. The PE department organized orienteering as well as other games to get the students out on to the downland immediately around the school. The French department took students to one of the major hotels to see aspects of local tourism. And so on. Wherever they went, the students' behaviour was immaculate, and the host adults were startled. Over and over again staff came back to school overjoyed at being able to repeat the compliments they had heard. 'Our students are the best-behaved they've ever had. They say we can go back at any time we like.'

All this did not happen in that first term; but the planning began, together with the change of attitude and expectation. Staff began to tell me about good times in the past. There had been a really successful Duke of Edinburgh Award Scheme in the school. 'I'll start it up again,' said the year head who had been involved before.

The students were so grateful to be given these chances that their delight was almost naïve. Many of them seemed to have gone without childhood, for all that their emotional development was in arrears. I encouraged staff to be creative in what they planned. I felt certain that this would help students to become academically more confident.

I was, though, up against the 'done-to' culture; years of being told that they were failing had made even the most successful teachers fearful of trying things out in response to what students seemed to need. I had to persuade them to trust my judgement, but I was aware that it might take years for this. I had all my independent experience to tell me there were no risks in the strategy. They had the burned-in memory of the brand 'Failure'.

Motivating students for learning

Planning student leadership

I also had copious experience of trusting students as leaders, at regular points in their schooling. I believed in making student leadership institutional, because school is a place where students amass experience as well as knowledge — in this instance, learning to become adults.

Students as leaders of their own learning

Most adults are sometimes guilty of discounting what children both experience and report; we see it as less valid than adult experience, tending to assume that 'growing up' means learning to discard juvenile ways of seeing the world. We now live with the converse, too: adolescent discounting of adult ways of seeing; massive commercial exploitation of adolescence. Media representations of how parents suffer during school holidays because of the expense, frustration and boredom of entertaining their children, do nothing to support the concept of adult and child learning together, or engaged in the processes that show children how to become adult. I felt that to change attitudes I would have to use media messages as well as making the point explicitly.

Subliminal messages

For instance, I posted on walls sayings or poems or ideas that would emphasize what I said in assemblies or staff meetings.

The students were highly entertained. 'What's she doing that for? What's that mean?' But they read them.

> I put Nelson Mandela's address on accepting the post of President of South Africa in the front entrance hall, because it had to be a headline. The key idea I wanted everyone to grasp was:
>
> Our deepest fear is not that we are inadequate.
>
> Our deepest fear is that we are powerful
> beyond measure.
>
> **It is our light, not our darkness, that most frightens us.**
>
> We ask ourselves, who am I to be brilliant,
> gorgeous, talented, fabulous?
>
> Actually, who are you not to be?
>
> You are a child of God. Your playing small
> doesn't serve the world.

There were lots about friendship, about ways of being together, because the students fought each other all the time. They brought the battles from neighbouring streets and from home into school.

I placed short poems everywhere, too. Poetry is one of the most powerful means for finding the order within emotional turbulence. And in any case, I loved it and wanted to share it. There was another poster about different learning styles, which I put all over the place — this was to help the staff, too, in case they forgot, under pressure, or in case students challenged a different way of managing a class.

I covered a wall with printouts of the PowerPoint slides I used in assembly to show their 'amazing brains': how London taxi drivers' brains have expanded in the area of visual-spatial development because of the feat of memory involved in 'The Knowledge;' the brain of a young boy who had reading problems, before and after spending time on intensive reading support: his brain now lit up in many areas. I wanted students to understand from the outset that I would never accept the plea,

'I can't.' I wanted to deter adults from saying, 'But children like those can't. . . '.

Preparation for leadership

By the end of the first term we had the kind of assembly I wanted. It seemed to take forever to get the students into the hall: the school hall, not the sports centre to which I was first introduced, without a PA system, with the opportunities to use lighting and presentation to create a magical atmosphere. I had not produced school plays and musicals for nothing. This was one of the rare situations where I put students into what could be interpreted as a submissive position: I wanted them sitting on the floor, with the staff around them. I wanted darkness, a focus on a lighted screen, amplified sound, dramatized gestures and concentration. I wanted to be sure that I could make eye contract with every one of them.

I wanted them to experience themselves as a community.

Every time, it worked. Staff would tell me that they could refer throughout the day to what was said in assembly. In these assemblies I could talk about what mattered to me; and try to authenticate what mattered to them.

Assembly like this only happened once a week because it made huge inroads into the curriculum time, but I thought it worth every moment of teaching 'lost'. I was preparing for students and staff to take the stage.

In schools where assemblies are taken very seriously, students and staff are much involved too. At WHS, the Head of Science demonstrated the reality of centripetal force and the awe and wonder of science by spinning the full bucket of water around her head in front of a crowded school. Collective bated breath and applause. Pupils eagerly seized the chance to speak for themselves. By my last couple of terms at Wimbledon, we could advertise The Soapbox: an opportunity for a pupil of any age to take the stage at assembly and tell us what she really thought about some controversial issue.

In Brighton, one of the high points for me is that a couple

of students progressed over a year from rejecting a microphone and reading from a scrappy piece of paper, to taking the microphone and speaking extempore for several minutes. We reached the situation where several students came to see me, just before the end of the summer term 2002. They wanted a change of time for the Final Awards Assembly. The Duke of Edinburgh contingent would be away for the last day, and they wanted to participate. I changed the date, even though it meant that I could not be present in the assembly because members of the Fresh Start unit were coming to visit.

That assembly ran for more than two hours, with crowds of students receiving awards or recreating scenes from the school drama production. I took the DfES officials into the back of the hall for a few minutes. They were deeply impressed. Staff were on hand to take charge if anything went wrong, but it did not. Afterwards, staff mused incredulously over the event — over the length of time in which all the students sat rapt and excited. The adults were stiff but exhilarated.

The Education Plan

Within a few weeks of beginning, I could write the Education Plan that spelt out the principles we would work with. It had to answer all the urgent questions related to an escalating budget deficit: being overstaffed and expecting the number of students to continue to decrease. The school had almost completely lost its shape. It needed to be reconstituted as a small, stable secondary school with an approach to student learning, curriculum development and staffing that could be sustained. I wanted us to have a foundation of principle that allowed us to predict our expenditure in a climate where governors could not know at the start of the academic year exactly how much money we would have.

The main elements of the plan were:

- **Emotional stability** and security. All the staff who stayed at the school had good relationships with the students and I wanted them to make full use of these, knowing what I do about how fear destabilizes learning. I planned to reorganize the school in all sorts of ways, following the logic of emotional security rather than conventional secondary school management.

- **Framework of values.** I believed that without some sort of underpinning spiritual, social, and cultural values, everyone would continue to feel embattled, worthless or victimised. I would make sure that time was spent on activities which might not appear to have immediate educational relevance, but which generated some of the spirituality embodied in Nelson Mandela's words.

- **Excited, creative learning**. I thought that much of what was usually taught was unimportant. I still think so. There is far too much in current education of what adults think children should know — an emphasis on passing on traditional information and values — when the only thing we can be certain about is that the children will need to learn things we cannot imagine or conceive. We need to teach them what they want to know about, so that they will be motivated to learn well and ambitiously. The passion for subject specialization is only useful if children are interested enough to become students. You can use almost any aspect of the curriculum to generate a love of learning.

- **A change of emphasis of teaching, from a subject basis to a learning basis.** Most of the Year 7 intake had not really finished primary school at all – either intellectually or emotionally. (This was later confirmed when a leading teacher from the primary phase joined the staff. She judged that the Year 7 students had the emotional development of Year 4 pupils.) There were so many problems in learning and behaviour that teachers needed to know individual students exceptionally well. If they taught them for more time in a week than is usual in secondary schools, they could tackle the profound learning problems. I wanted students to be taught several subjects by the same teacher — midway between primary and secondary practice. This would allow staff realistically to follow what individual students were doing, from how they learned to whether or not they came to school. Instead of trying to manage the learning of between two and four hundred students each week — the classic secondary school model — they would work with a relatively small number, so that they could concentrate on how students learn.

- **Preparation to become a school of the future.** I was sure that in future schools, teachers would specialize in learning, not subject knowledge. Adopting a more flexible, creative approach would require us to find new structures for leadership, new ways of teaching. We would be preparing the school for the future rather than just trying to catch up with everyone else.

- **Assessment of the whole child's performance, rather than aspects of the child.** Primary school teachers are able to work closely together far more easily than secondary school staff for reasons already given. The College of Media Arts staff needed to develop their professional collaboration as fast as possible because there was no deep-seated culture of learning in the school. This culture has to be made first and foremost by the adults. It is like discipline, which is the collective sense of purpose in the adult community, not a set of rules.

- **Mutual accountability.** In the short term, I wanted to change the school organization so that teachers did not expect that supply staff would take their classes if they were absent. If everyone taught a bit less, whilst it would seem on the face of it to be more expensive, we could cover for one another's absences instead of paying for supply teachers. This was to ensure that students only ever met staff they already knew and respected. They would gradually lose the habit of disruption. At the same time, staff would learn what happened in other people's lessons, and would, also gradually, begin to develop a sense that they were accountable to one another.

I knew the governors would be happy about these plans; I felt confident HMI would, too; and I was used to having to account for my work to GDST officers, although educational judgements from independent school heads are rarely questioned if they seem to make business sense.

The new factor for me was that other agencies seemed to think they should have their say: Fresh Start unit; LEA. The LEA Assistant Director of Education, responsible for School Effectiveness, was someone with whom I had instantly fallen into dialogue. She not only understood and approved, but also found the primary school teacher for us.

As I started implementing the plan other agencies suddenly appeared: Education Action Zone, teacher unions, Youth Offending Team, New Deal for Communities. The New Deal was another government initiative, through which depressed and possibly downtrodden communities were given enormous funding (millions of pounds) over a 20-year period in order to regenerate themselves. They had to match their grant with equivalent millions of pounds from business partners. What interested me in this initiative was the time-scale: 20 years for regeneration, as against 3 years for Fresh Start schools. There were several LEA advisers, not just from Brighton but from West Sussex. I discovered that money had been spent in purchasing additional advice from this other LEA. The advisers were very good, but I was puzzled about the assumption that this hard-pressed budget had already been allocated to fees outside the school instead of to salaries for staff who would actually teach in the school.

However, I got the benefit of the doubt in the short term; schools in Special Measures are protected — or confined — by the decisions of the Monitoring Inspector. Our HMI, Colin Humphries, was outstanding.

Making things happen

I wish I could convey the sense of intense exhilaration and concentration in which I lived for months on end. It was as if the very ends of my hair were aware. Derek Bown would often stick his head around the door. 'Problems in the Maths corridor. You ought to get down there.'

'Looking good, Jill. Some good lessons.'

'You're having fun, aren't you?'

I was. I loved every minute of it. I loved the fact that the students responded, that the staff began to smile, that I could see and report on good teaching. At the end of the first term we placed an advertisement in the *Evening Argus*, announcing that the school would be open for a week for visitors. I called it 'An Awfully Big Adventure' because I wanted to capitalize on the novelty of the dreaded place confidently inviting everyone within its walls. Hardly anyone came, but the students astonished the staff by behaving well and by competing to show round their guests.

Defining the independence of a school

Increasingly, though, I found that I needed to assert the independence of the school in ways I did not anticipate. The simplest way of describing this is to explain how the New Deal for Communities drew up its *Six Themes for East Brighton*. In this published document were targets for school attendance, school attainment, reducing bullying and so forth. The school had not been consulted about this at all. I marvelled at the innocence of these planners. How did they think anyone from outside a school could seriously influence attendance or attainment without either working inside, or through, the school?

The boundary between school and community

I tackled the issue about bullying first, because it was easy to explain.

New Deal for Communities, it transpired, would pay for an expert who would instruct the staff on how to deal with bullying, because the staff, obviously, did not know how. I explained our policy and practice and suggested the budget should be given to the school so that we would have more resources for managing the problem. Perhaps those who managed bullying on the estate should meet those who evolved the school policy, so that we could try to use the same language and the same methods. Students who bullied at school, and adolescents who bullied on the estate — or their parents — would understand that school and the local community worked together.

Most staff were good at managing bullying situations in school; others were outstandingly good. We knew we could not eliminate bullying without transforming the world outside, which was beyond our remit. Effective schools know the difference between managing a situation and transforming it. We might prevent a student from exercising bullying strategies in school; but we could not change the bully's desire for power unless we thought we were capable of managing his/her life experiences.

Help for the principal in maintaining the boundary

I had a developed sense of what was 'proper' and 'improper' in the relationship between schools and outside agencies; this had grown through my being in effective schools for most of my professional life. In the course of my first term at the College of Media Arts I began to get angry. For a long time, anger was energizing. I began to see that outside agencies of all kinds had not just failed the students and their families, but had colluded at sustaining the conditions for failure. I expected to talk on equal terms with everyone outside the school — and indeed, this did happen for much of the time; but in crucial areas I could feel a great pressure from without to make the school conform in some way. I was not sure about how it was to conform; I just knew I was not going to let this happen. I found myself repeatedly asserting the boundary between the school and what was outside, because only from within could the real, long-term changes come.

I chose to go back to The Grubb Institute for mentoring of the most taxing kind. I wanted to make sure that anything I thought or planned was subjected to rigorous and unremitting comment. Bruce Reed, founder of the Institute, was by then in his early 80s. He had a formidable intellect, and was a radical social thinker. For the better part of a year, I chose professional development under his guidance; what's more, it was free. Bruce wanted me to experience one of the key learning protocols used at The Institute to see if I was willing to join its council as a trustee.

This discipline ensured that I could never deceive myself, which was what I wanted to guarantee. There were times when the effort of going to London at the end of a long school day for a two-hour session with Bruce was daunting; but invariably I was invigorated by the insights I gained. Although I attended many meetings of headteachers in Brighton, none of them had Bruce's professional sharpness and relevance of conversation.

Talking to Bruce had enabled me to think about the school in relation to the community, as well as in terms of its own structure and function, so that I saw the need for defining appropriate boundaries. The conversation about managing bullying rapidly took a positive turn, once both parties realized we wanted something practical to happen. Within the New Deal was a Community Safety Team of police and neighbourhood wardens, whose work was focused on the Whitehawk estate. The leader of the team was a former student of Stanley Deason High School; he was a university graduate and a tremendous role model.

Together, we arrived at a definition of 'community' that was going to serve whenever there was a threat of bullying, sexual harassment, substance misuse or anything else of concern. Even though there were plenty of students in the school who did not live on the Whitehawk estate, and the school was not located in the estate, everyone who attended the school was to be considered as part of the community. The Community Safety Team had licence to deal with any situation in our community, once we invited them in.

When we excluded students, we would tell the Community Safety Team; if someone in the school threatened to 'get you on the way home,' we could ring the Community Safety Team. Not only would neighbourhood wardens escort a threatened student home, if necessary, but one of the police team would go to visit the bully at home, too. In short, we would make it impossible for any student in the school to feel that staff would be unable to do anything about threats uttered at school but carried out somewhere else.

A model for collaboration

This model of joint working gave me great hope that it would be possible to build up similar patterns with all the other agencies. There was something deeply pragmatic and good-humoured about it all: we were dealing with specific children and their families; there were plenty of ideas. The Community Safety Team was itself an innovation, trying to find ways of working that would be trustworthy and would generate trust. I trusted everyone in that team; I believed that they trusted us.

Establishing systems: finding and using information to help students succeed

From the very beginning I struggled to discover what students were capable of and could do, because there was so little information of the kind I was used to working with. Whilst there was plenty about levels of literacy (depressing: by the end of my first term I worked out that the average reading age of Year 10 students was 11. Their average chronological age would be about 15) there was scarcely anything about ability. Key Stage results give very few clues. It was obvious from the disturbed behaviour everywhere that there must be not just significant specific learning difficulties and complex social problems, but also lots of discrepancies: frustrated students who could not adjust to the boring curriculum; talents which found no outlets at school; students who were musical, artistic, quietly ingenious, struggling to express themselves in writing but sensitive and logical in speech. There was nothing at all to identify the obviously gifted. I discovered entirely by accident that there was a boy of 15 who already had a scratch handicap at golf and was likely to play for the England junior team.

The maxim I brought with me from the independent sector — that no student could be allowed to fail — would be hard to hold to if we had scant knowledge of how to help each child to hope, in ways which matched the child's own dreams.

Chapter 5

Term 2: Summer 2001

Planning for Special Educational Needs

Assuming such students can succeed

By the end of my first term, I had a clear idea about what needed to be done, and set about canvassing ideas, advice and support from external agencies that only they could provide. There were a number of students in the school who ought not to be in mainstream education — not, that is, without lifestyle support of a kind I knew teachers could not offer. They needed different experiences from those given to most students; intensive education so that they could relearn responses; it was as if they needed to destroy some brain pathways in order to make fresh ones.

Calling the external agencies for help: Meeting One — planning NOT to exclude

I invited representatives from many different agencies to meet me, among them the school doctor and school nurse (we had the standard allocation of a nurse for a day a week); community liaison workers; social services; the Child and Adolescent Mental Health Services; and the Alternative Centre for Education (ACE:

the newly-created Brighton facility for supporting students with Emotional and Behavioural Difficulties). School staff were there too.

I had a simple purpose: these were students heading for permanent exclusion; I did not want to exclude them. How could we all work together so that they could stay in school successfully to complete their education?

Almost everyone representing an external agency pleaded special circumstances: their own limited budget; their own targets; other demands on them. Everyone round the table knew that these students must be among the most challenging in the city; but nothing was going to be done. We were on our own — a situation I had come to expect. Agencies would tell you what to do and expect you to do it, but could/would not become practically involved themselves. It was a very dispiriting meeting.

However, in preparing for the meeting I had gathered an enormous amount of information. I felt I had a really good grasp of the kinds of problems we faced, the students and their families faced, and the current educational strategies for dealing with them.

Calling the external agencies for help: Meeting Two — planning success for disillusioned students

A few weeks later I called another meeting, to garner ideas on how to work with older students who were also at risk: not just the disruptive, but the quiet ones who might give up on their own education. Sometimes they would sit at the back of a class doing nothing, learning nothing. Sometimes they would be gently disruptive; sometimes they simply did not come to school at all. I recalled all those students I had met in other schools who could not identify themselves with the mainstream curriculum — and yet who, given some experiences and opportunities, could really love learning something. That was all I wanted: that they should love learning something and be prepared to work at it.

Although a large number of people turned up unexpectedly

at this meeting, only one of them came with immediate, practical suggestions and the willingness to work inside the school. He had just been appointed as consultant in the Education Action Zone, to focus on the two high schools in the Zone (the other was Falmer High) — and his ideas were invigorating. I had already been doing some research and he was prepared to carry on with it. He was one of very few from outside who were prepared to work over a sustained period of time with students and to have his work inspected.

At this meeting I discovered just how much money some other agencies possessed, which was not going to be focused through the school. The Youth Offending Team had money it could use with students who had been brought before the courts. These funds could only be used outside of the school. This was just one example. I had now been six months at the school and I was beginning to tire of this repeated discovery — there was money in abundance, but not in schools or under the control of schools. Whereas in the independent sector all the available money was concentrated in the school and at the disposal of the governors and headteacher, in the maintained sector the money was distributed among many different agents. I would just have used it all to employ more adults in the school, all working together, focused on a single aim: giving students good experiences of learning.

A year later our consultant was asking if there would be a job at the school for him. The EAZ was being wound down and he would need to look for work. He really wanted to join the team. We had a place for him but no money. Of course, he rapidly found a promoted post in another secondary school.

One of the more frustrating aspects of this meeting was that I brought to it information I had gathered at a conference organized by the Home Office on how to deal with truancy and crime by improving school attendance. I had met headteachers from other areas in the country who had exciting ideas to offer, such as the establishment of separate and really high-quality facilities for disaffected young people. They had evidence that by inventive and detailed attention to individual needs, it was possible to encourage high levels of attendance and interest. I talked about this, but what I said was largely ignored. I kept the ideas in mind, even so.

Independent planning

Throughout the Summer Term 2001, I was coming to terms with what it meant to lead a maintained school that needed radical approaches if it were to succeed. There could be no sustained help with the very damaged students because resources outside the school were already committed. This seemed to be related to the LEA's management plan. The available advice, especially from the Chief Educational Psychologist, was very good but deeply depressing. I started talking to him on a regular basis so that I would understand the underlying issues. The new educational psychologist at ACE said that she could not see anywhere in Brighton any resources for dealing with these children. I had lunch on a regular basis with the Head of ACE so that I could connect what he planned and intended with what we planned at school. I tried to find and use the expertise that was outside the school as well as inside it, so that I could make the best-informed judgements possible in the circumstances.

Liaison with local headteachers

There was little support from the other Brighton headteachers. My main ally was the headteacher of Falmer High School. Anthony Edkins rapidly let me know what I would find from my fellow heads. We took to going together to the joint meetings, so that we could talk things over afterwards. He warned me that I would be entering a battleground. I had already discovered at an Admissions meeting that we were not operating in a comprehensive system but a free market.

Anthony would say, 'The other heads are terrified in case Comart or Falmer close and then they'll have to have our kids in their schools.'

The alternative curriculum

There were few resources for establishing an alternative curriculum for students who might exclude themselves from education, although there were some good ideas; and I was beginning to understand how the New Deal for Communities should work. I spent much of the Summer Term getting out into the community, to meet as many people and agencies as I could. I was looking for more resources.

I discovered a heading in the school budget called Work Related Learning. 'What's that?' 'Oh,' said Kathy Stonier, 'this is the last year of it. It pays for some students to go to City College for their hairdressing course. That sort of thing.' There was £25,000 in the budget for the last year. Some of it was committed to funding courses, but the rest would pay for an adult, not a teacher: someone who wanted to work with young people, who could spend time with a selected group working in the school for realistic qualifications that they wanted to achieve.

We were overwhelmed by the applications: the sheer number of people who wanted the same chance to make a difference. Our EAZ consultant organized the workplace learning, the qualifications and the timetable. He set time aside to work personally with some of the students. We had a rational, coherent programme for the following year — one where we would not react to crisis, but choose students for a new way of working. We could then plan something more permanent to take its place.

Planning NOT to exclude: providing for students at risk

My attempts to appoint a nurse ran aground on the plans laid in the EAZ to fund a school counsellor. I was unable to persuade the EAZ to put funds into our budget towards a nurse, instead, so had to await the arrival of a counsellor. One was finally appointed early in 2003; more than two years after the plans were first made, even though the funding had always been available.

I made other arrangements for September 2001, finding some welfare assistants to act as first port of call for distressed students. We were trying to produce an integrated plan — the new staff were to work differently with students who earlier were either excluded or sent to the Time Out room to cool off. I was impatient because the students' needs were now, not in some bureaucratic time-scale. In the independent sector, once we identified a need we acted on it. It was dishonest to do otherwise.

I continued to meet regularly with the Chief Educational Psychologist; if we could not appoint a nurse who understood mental health issues, perhaps another professional could help: an educational psychologist. We were free to use what was left from the Fresh Start funding for this, and struck an agreement to split a salary between the Educational Psychology service and the school.

When she arrived, our new educational psychologist would not just assess students judged to have special educational needs; she would work alongside staff to advise them. She had specialized skills for dealing with traumatized students; there were so many of these in the school that all staff were teachers of students with SEN; not just a dedicated few.

Developing internal capacity: the growth of staff self-confidence

We consciously started to use the potential of staff to teach one another.

Staff came forward for new posts of responsibility that fitted the school structure we were trying to evolve for ourselves. Others planned a new Personal Development programme, which everyone would teach from September 2001. Staff began to behave as confident professionals, rather than as dependent apprentices.

Partnership with new media industries

Some of the new media business people had bad memories of school themselves, and were sympathetic to the students. The head of a dynamic new firm, Worth Media, which brought together a wide range of professionals, from software specialists to psychologists, visited the school, recognized what was happening and offered detailed partnership.

We began to think differently about literacy and the place of visual intelligence. We saw that even the most truculent students were not just adept users of new technology, but willing to learn. Reluctant readers would ask for the meaning of words on a screen that they would not consider reading aloud from a book. The potential for learning in the proposed Media Arts specialization became clearer and a group of staff started working together on the strategy for the future. In the short term, they designed a simple and more integrated approach for teaching the new Year 7 students in September 2001, which would enhance the primary school approach we would start to adopt.

Networking locally: Brighton City Forum

Brighton City Forum had been created by Anthony Seldon, Headmaster of Brighton College, and Douglas McKittrick, the Vicar of Brighton, for people who led institutions in the city to debate ideas about the future.

Anthony and Douglas were very good hosts. I met the potential sponsor for the College of Media Arts as an Academy there (the government having stipulated that schools wishing to acquire academy status should find independent sponsorship of £2 million, before the government would supply funding); and the local controller of BBC Southern Counties who realised that I was desperate for a radio station for the students. I listened to the Bishop of Oxford conjuring up an image of 'The Good City' and longed to play my part too. I realized that there were many professionals in the city who were eager to help the school, but who could find no structure for doing so, since they were not going to send their children there. I understood why.

Such initiatives were under our control. We relied on no external agency to help us tackle some of the most serious problems in the school. Once we had demonstrated that we could set up and use good systems for planning and monitoring new work, other professionals were relieved to work alongside us.

But I began to feel that this was not enough. In my first headship, one of the key issues was that teaching staff had contracts of employment fitted for day schools, not boarding schools. Eventually, I persuaded the governors to offer new contracts to the staff, giving higher salaries in exchange for commitment to some of the contingencies of boarding school life. I wanted to ensure that staff deployment would fit student need and parental expectation.

Alliance with major institutions

My first instinct was that the only way in which potential parents in Brighton would begin to change their assumptions about the school was if one of the country's great institutions was willing to stand alongside the school community. I did not know at the time that Stanley Deason had formed a similar view — and he had the political will and influence to establish the school. His vision for the young people in the deprived parts of East Brighton saw education from early years onwards as a vital force in transforming their lives; and he called upon the politicians and lawyers he knew for support.

I felt the school ought to be independent of the local authority, because there were too many political pressures in the city for the needs of the students to be considered justly. Students needed to be viewed inside a value system that placed spirituality first: I wanted them to know that in the eye of God each student was unique and essential in our society. I wanted them to feel that their local community was the whole city of Brighton, not just the Whitehawk estate or its like. The notion of 'community' embodied in 'community school' was deceptive in ways I wanted to challenge. If the community is in itself deprived; if its inhabitants feel excluded; if they act as scapegoats, representing the dark side of human experience, then 'their' community school will carry the same burden of exclusion and inadequacy.

It seemed too risky to attach hope to one strategy alone, so I pursued several at once which I thought could be linked; and of course, I talked about everything to Derek Bown, as ideas arose. His deep knowledge of education and politics, his combination of scepticism and faith in human potential, combined with his wicked sense of humour, made him a formidable campaigner. Kathy Stonier completed this triangle. She was developing fast the skills needed for headship and had strongly independent feelings and judgements of her own.

None of these actions would necessarily have any immediate relevance to freeing the school from Special Measures. I was trying to think ahead about a framework for the future that would ensure the school never went back into Special Measures — and, far more important, that the students' experience of school would be similar to what the majority of children would hope for. I wanted that hope to be felt by teachers, too. The school had to be attractive to exciting teachers.

Looking for partners in initiative

The business partner: Asda

At Brighton Marina was a large and expanding Asda store, which served not just the local community of Whitehawk, but the affluent inhabitants of the expensive new houses and flats, and the international contingent which anchored in the Marina itself. This was Asda at its most representative.

I talked to the General Manager about creating a partnership. Staff could discover the management skills and tactics of other institutions; there could be training opportunities not just for staff but for students; Asda could reduce its shoplifting problem; the school could find a venue not just for publicity but for meeting parents.

Uniform: chosen from Asda, by the students on the College Council

I wanted to relaunch school uniform, chosen by the College Council, from Asda's regular clothing range. This might convince staff and students alike that student leadership was real. But Asda philosophy for stocking shelves was at odds with the kind of stability that schools need. Parents rang the school in frustration because the suggested uniform was not in stock, and there was no intention that it should be. 'Rollback' policy at Asda prevents any such assurance. The Asda General Manager had not really grasped the implications of becoming the official uniform supplier for a school.

Asda's 'Rollback' policy relies for success on short-term response, minimal stock in the store, replenishment according to the status of the demand. Schools rely on long-term planning and response. Sometimes, you will not know that an educational strategy has worked until twenty years later. Schools need huge reserves of social, emotional and intellectual capital which they hold all the time. They do not stock ideas or information on the 'just in time' principle. They create the culture on which their students draw. In long-established schools, each incomer is taught something fundamental about 'the way it is.'

The partnership with Asda petered out because the General Manager expected to move from Brighton as his career developed. Other students in school were incredulous that the Council's choices had been accepted. They had so little experience of student decisions being taken seriously that they had not really bothered to make their feelings known to their Council representatives. They were more used to students who exercised power, through personal dominance, than to students who worked with authority through taking up roles, such as being elected to a student council. It would take a great deal of persistence on my part to convince staff and students to commit themselves to the experiment of trusting students to find and use authority.

What did I learn about uniform?

It was easy for someone from a middle-class background, as they perceived me, to recommend a uniform from Asda. They associated Asda with their own experience. They felt that everyone else in society saw their experience and values as invalid. Asking them to wear uniform from Asda was inviting them to accept that they were from an underclass.

I should have used the Fresh Start money to buy very high status uniform and given it free to everyone because too many of the families could not have afforded it. I know this would have caused innumerable problems, but I expect I would have found a way of managing this.

Frankly, I do not care a fig for uniform. I cannot see how a focus on clothing — or hair — or jewellery — assists in the process of learning. But in this context, I was willing to talk about the role of uniform in establishing identity. I talked to the school about uniformed organizations which were trusted: firemen; armed forces; nurses. Issuing a very expensive uniform could have carried another message: 'You are important and trusted.' It would have been novel.

Spirituality: alliance with the Diocese of Chichester

In the tiny Whitehawk Parish Church one Sunday afternoon in June 2001, I met the new Bishop of Chichester, John Hind. He said, perhaps as people do in such circumstances, 'If there's anything I can do, please let me know.' I went home thinking furiously and sent him a letter. Lord Dearing, former chief executive of the Post Office, chair of numerous academic and business organizations and of commissions of inquiry, notably into higher education (1996–1997) had recently published a report on Church of England schools (2001), in which he suggested an expansion of Christian secondary schools. He wrote movingly about the church's mission to serve those in the most deprived areas of society. I asked Bishop John for help.

This set us off on a series of discussions, involving Douglas McKittrick, and the Diocesan Director of Education, Jeremy Taylor. The Diocese had no Anglican secondary school in the area and was willing to work toward the transformation of East Brighton. John Hind was not going to be sidetracked by the ancestral image of establishment, political appointment of bishops, the social fabric of stable middle-class England. The Diocese was prepared to be a partner, finding someone who would work as chaplain to the school. Douglas thought he could find a Rabbi, an Imam, a Buddhist leader, and a Roman Catholic priest, willing to come into the school to be with the students and staff. We did not think it would be difficult to achieve.

Independence: the Academy unit

I had stayed in touch with Angela Rumbold, who started talking to me about the Academy programme. I really knew very little about it, but Angela was intimately involved with Church Schools Company — a group of independent schools somewhat similar to the Girls' Day Schools Trust, which had revisited its social purpose and decided to try to set up a network of academies around the country, which would work together and in parallel with the independent schools. A separate United Learning Trust (ULT) had been established, with Angela as its Chair. We arranged for her to visit the College of Media Arts and I started investigating academies.

As the end of the Summer Term 2001 approached I was acutely aware of the importance of the new term.

Visits from Her Majesty's Inspectors

Each term, our Monitoring Inspector visited the school with another colleague for two days. He went everywhere. We gave him copious information each time, especially after he told us that he knew we would not be able to show evidence of measurable improvement through GCSE or Key Stage results. He well understood the school's position, and often pondered how he could write his reports on these monitoring visits in order to point up the inadequacies of the LEA, as he saw them. HMI reports were not meant to include such comments.

His advice helped us to set in motion a rolling programme for Work Scrutiny, where work was gathered which would represent a term's learning. We were looking at evidence in books as well as in lessons that students had actually learned and were making improvements.

At the end of the Summer Term in 2001 he told me that he

understood how much rested on the plans I was making for the school. There were no 'quick fixes' in what I was doing. He understood that everything was systemic, deep-seated, radical in the original sense of the word.

Recently I found an image to explain what I was trying to do when putting plans into practice. I was training for a half marathon, tripped and fell comprehensively, gouging a deep wound in the palm of my hand, that required a visit to the local casualty department. The wound had be dressed and checked by a nurse, who, after several visits, asked a doctor to look at it. The wound still looked stark and unpleasant. 'Ah yes,' said the doctor. 'It's granulating nicely. No problems there.' Granulating? I enquired. The wound was healing from within, and invisibly except to an expert eye.

Our Inspector said he would return early in the Autumn Term to see what was happening, since these plans were so important.

PFI

In the meantime, Kathy Stonier and I struggled to make sense of plans presented by the competitor PFI firms. There were now only two bidders left, since once had withdrawn, and, of the two plans, one demonstrated educational insight and the other did not. We wanted to vote for the first bidder, but suspected the second would be more popular with the other schools. Whatever the outcome, we had to be sure of that the plans were sensible — but at the same time, we could not reveal the plans of one to the other.

Instead, we walked around the school site with the architects from Jarvis (who ultimately were awarded the PFI contract), to explain in detail why their plans were inadequate. It was disconcerting to hear that they recognized this but had simply failed to take into account the financial implications of redesigning the plans so that they were sensible. In effect, they proposed a brand new building at the end of the site, more or less as a fourth box added to the three already existing boxes. The only sensible solution would be to redesign all the corridors in the main buildings, and to reorder classrooms and other facilities, so that the new media arts building would be integrated with the whole instead of simply adding to the problems.

In order to present a coherent plan, Jarvis had to cut costs in their proposed building to allow for the financial impact of the other work they knew would be essential. Kathy and I pored over ground-plans of the current and proposed buildings, so that our suggestions would help them. We felt that we had to explain fundamental issues about how schools run. We also profoundly hoped that the other bidder would win the contract, but suspected that we would be outvoted by the other three schools.

The LEA had appointed a team of staff to work with the bidders, arranging meetings for all the headteachers, and any staff they appointed to help them, with architects and designers. Derek Bown and I wearily and warily attended these, although I tried hard not to let myself spend time and energy on the plans.

The decision would ultimately be taken by the schools together with the LEA advisory team, and the latter would be engaged in working out which of the bidders would provide the best value for money. A governor at one of the other schools canvassed us with information about the unreliability of PFI contracts; and the governors of the College of Media Arts anxiously debated how we would pay our share of the costs, because they were all to be based on a completely unrealistic estimate of the number of students in the school. This number had been given to the bidders by the LEA: 950 students in 5 years' time. I embarked on a fruitless battle to persuade the LEA team to revise this number significantly downwards. I thought it would be hugely difficult just to reach 700 students on roll in 5 years.

Chapter 6

Term 3: Autumn 2001

Plans in practice

School reopened with a new sense of concentration. There were the usual problems of long-term staff absence, but even the supply teachers were positive. Instead of this being the school every teacher dreaded being sent to, we were told that others in the city were worse. It was a curious compliment.

With a clear philosophical framework and straightforward, practical approaches, the plans were working. One of the most entertaining moments of the mid-term visit from Colin Humphries, our HMI, was his encounter with our newly-recruited ex-primary school teacher. Rebecca had been a source of enormous encouragement. She had instantly identified her Year 7 class as having the emotional and social development appropriate to Year 4. She brought primary school planning methods into the secondary framework — plans allowing flexibility, and attention to individual needs. She wanted to redesign teaching rooms to give them a primary school aspect. She was burstingly confident and freely critical. Colin entered my study with a quizzical look.

He had been tackled by Rebecca. Why had he not been to see her and to inspect the books of her students to see their progress?

She had taken him firmly aside to show what he should be inspecting, and expecting. This was the professional confidence and skill he wanted to see.

At the end of the visit, he said he would return at the start of the Spring Term 2002, in the hope of removing the school from Special Measures. It was a vote of confidence that kept us going when things got tough.

Attendance problems

One problem we seemed unable to change: attendance. An expensive electronic registration system called Bromcom had been installed in January 2001. It gave enormous amounts of data on student attendance at all classes, but, as is often the case when people have to get to grips with new software, there were start-up problems.

We did our best to use and analyse the information. The assistant principal in charge of attendance spent many hours late into the evening staring at a computer screen, trying to track the attendance of individual students who had been given targets for improvement. The Education Welfare Officers (EWOs) visited homes, met parents or carers and tried to persuade them to support school attendance. There were the usual excuses.

— *How can I make her go? I go to work and she says she's going and then I get home and she says she's had a headache.*

— *He says he's being bullied so he has to wait for me to come home from work so I can walk him to the school.*

— *I've not been well so I needed her to stay home to look after Kylie for me.*

— *It's got nothing to do with me.*

The EWO would arrange to fetch the student every day, if it was practicable. Sometimes we tried sending a taxi, though this was horribly expensive. In the previous Summer Term I had joined one EWO on her 'doorstepping' trail to locate students and their parents. I knew that other schools would pay students to come to school. I could not do this: how could I tell students that they had amazing brains and deserved the best if I was also bribing others to come to school?

In November the national Attendance Tables were published. The College of Media Arts was at the bottom and once again I was besieged by press phone calls.

It was frustrating to spend energy on the negative just at the point when I was beaming out buoyancy and encouragement to everyone. I hated to sound as if I was justifying our position, in pointing out that the tables were based on calculations including all students — which meant the invisible cohort whom no one had seen for months or years.

The most constructive response was from Joanne Good, who ran the daily BBC Southern Counties Breakfast show in Brighton. I went into the studio, as I often did, to answer her questions. She was invariably sympathetic and interested. Off air, she talked about harnessing the glamour of Brighton celebrities to try to encourage students to come to school. I went away hopeful again.

We needed these votes of confidence because some of the problems we encountered were so stark. I am including two at length as typical, to show just what some children have to confront.

Special needs: exclusion

Within two weeks of the academic year's beginning (September 2001), I find myself seated beside an 11 year-old-boy who has already proved to be violently disruptive and difficult. He runs away from adults who address him in the mildest of tones. His lighters and matches have been removed. He has found and kept a knife in school. He abuses his peers and walks both out of lessons and into them (not his own) banging doors and shouting abuse. He is with me for two reasons: he is unsafe — he will not follow the most basic of instructions which could keep him secure in the school building — and he has tied together the gates of the Astroturf on which a class had a physical education lesson. He used his shoelaces. The only way the teacher could escape was by finding someone from outside willing to cut the laces. There is a certain humour in this, and I make a mental note of his ingenuity.

I have summoned his grandfather to see me, to explain why I am excluding this boy for a short fixed term of a few days. The boy looks very small, thin and pale. As soon as his grandfather is in the room, he can only look sideways, sliding his glance, at him, not at me. Actually, although the records from the previous school talk about this man as his grandfather they say that he is also probably the father. The year head, a tough, experienced and skilful teacher has already given me a wry account of his several encounters with (grand)father.

I want the boy to understand how important it is that he should obey me; if he won't follow my instructions as head-teacher, no adult can expect to have authority. I also want to give this boy a sense of authority as being calm, just and certain. Any child in this school refusing to obey a reasonable instruction can expect to be excluded from it for a fixed period of days. By 'reasonable' I mean requests such as: 'I know you are upset; come and sit with me for a moment.' 'I know you are angry; please come out of this classroom — which isn't yours — and talk to Mr Smith. I know you get on with him.'

I have taken this stance because of the locked doors everywhere in the school, which I want to open. We have to carry massive bunches of keys to get from one part of the building to another. A few children inhabit the corridors — an alternative homeland which they roam around as if on an island all their own, with secret tracks and hiding places. They cannot stay in a classroom, however wonderful the teaching.

Kathy Stonier, the vice-principal, is with me. Forewarned by the year head we do not intend to meet this man alone. The boy cannot hear what I say; he cannot understand or even sense the idea I want to give him of other adults in the world being trustworthy. He has eyes only for his (grand)father, a red-faced, stocky, ferociously upright figure who seems desperate for the boy to attend school and to learn. He says, 'Are you listening to me? If you don't do what Miss tells you I'll come up here and beat you in front of her. Do you hear me? If she has to ring me about you, I'll come up here and beat you in front of her.' Kathy and I try not to catch each other's eye; instead, I look for a private word with the boy. I do not want him walking away with the expectation that we will condone beatings. But I can't easily challenge it at the moment because we want the boy to do some work whilst he is at home, and we need cooperation. We make a note — this may be a family we need to refer to Social Services in due course.

When the boy returns from his fixed term exclusion, I catch him in a corridor. 'Listen,' I say, vainly, 'I don't want to have to ring your grandfather. If you feel you are going to lose control, you only have to go and find Mr Smith and it will be OK. It's over, now. We'll start again. Did you get on with the work we set you to do at home?'

I can't tell whether or not he believes me or even hears what I say; but I say it even so, because I know that I have to keep repeating the same simple statements about what the school values. A year later, I sit before a Governors' Disciplinary Panel explaining why I am asking for my permanent exclusion of this student to be upheld. It is.

The governors are deeply sympathetic to the school's plight. We have tried everything we know. The Education Welfare Officer, who has been supporting the family, and I have discussed how to help the boy from every angle we know. He concludes that at least with a permanent exclusion the boy will have to be supported by what the legislation states. I already know that the outside agencies will be unable to help in any way that's effective; but school has to be safe for everyone else, too.

I have discovered that the local education authority will ignore our experience with this child, and our naïve hope that he will be assigned to the intensive care of a special school. Although the boy now has a Statement of Special Educational Need, he will be sent to another mainstream school. He has 'entitlement' to a place in a mainstream school because that is what Inclusion is interpreted as meaning.

But we have seen how this boy has been brought up. Whenever his (grand)father is in the room, it's as if he is hypnotized. He cannot make eye contact with anyone else. I am told that if he could spend all day constructing models from kits, he would be happy. I remember the boy who tied the gates together with his shoelaces, thereby causing much concealed amusement as well as irritation to the teacher in charge. This child isn't malevolent. The continual setting of fires which has been one of his pastimes is not, I think, malicious but experimental. Despite everything he is an innocent still.

I would be happy, actually, if he were making models. I think he'd learn. He'd start to ask questions. He might start to design the kits for himself. But he would need a dedicated adult setting very clear boundaries for his world; he'd need to spend time in a high-dependency unit such as we find in hospitals today — and it would have to be a total environment to change the patterns of neural networks made by his experiences so far. But there is no institution, it seems, willing and able to provide the holistic and imaginative environment in which this child can relearn the responses to the world that make him impossible to contain. In fact, we are supposed to be doing our best by him by reinserting him into the mainstream somewhere else.

I drive to his home late one evening to deliver the formal and final notification of permanent exclusion. (Grand)father comes out to greet me and is polite, concerned, troubled for his child. He suddenly seems like a perfectly normal parent. We stand in the evening sunlight talking idly for a couple of minutes and I see him as loving and baffled.

We cannot contain this child any longer, partly because there are so many like him in the school; but we had hoped that something better might have been planned for him as a result of the exclusion. The EWO is not hopeful about this, though. His experiences of multi-agency working are similar to mine; like me, he wants to work in a completely different way; he is frustrated by the conventional approaches to Welfare.

I have come to understand why any request such as 'please come here to talk to me' is not perceived by some of my students as reasonable. We speak from different worlds. Nonetheless, I am trying to convince them that *my* world is the normal, day-to-day world of affection, stability, hope for the future, recognition of talent, realizable ambition, aspiration, social confidence.... And I know some of the history which makes them cynical, unable to imagine or conceive what I am attempting to describe.

Two months later, I sit again, in September (2002), with a thin, pale 11 year-old boy who after a week in school, has proved to be dangerous. He patiently explains to me that he has learned from his father how to be violent. He is a dear little boy, intelligent and honest in his eagerness to explain that it took years for his father to beat the violence into him. He tells me that his father left the home three years earlier, but he can feel the effects in him now, still.

His older sister has already been at the school for a couple of years. She solves her problems by hugging the staff, including me. She too is tiny. An older stepsister was one of the first students I had to exclude from the school in Year 11 as someone so aggressively uncontrollable that we could not stop her. It was a fixed term exclusion but she did not return: another non-attender for the statistics.

The Child Protection record on this family makes grim reading. Within a month or so our Year 7 child and another younger sibling are in foster care. He is tremendously proud of this and tells everyone. But his problems have not been resolved. He still has a desperate need for adult attention and affection. If someone can set him small tasks all day long — stuffing envelopes, carrying messages — he is delighted and delightful. His intelligence is transparent. Somehow, despite everything else, he has excellent powers of observation and reasoning. But if he feels upset, he will walk out of the school, causing a major scare as we try to locate him.

Very often these children are pale, thin, wiry with energy of a dysfunctional kind: it is a deep and unfocused anger. Breakfast is not usually part of their known world and they won't come to a breakfast club either. It smacks of institution, and these children are deeply suspicious of anything beyond what they know.

Systems to answer special needs

These are just two stories, but I could tell a multitude. When I began at the school I asked for specifics. 'Tell me who are the most difficult; and why; and let's work out what we can do for them before they explode and we have to exclude them.' It seemed sensible enough to think out a strategy in advance. I was told about 55 students, from an official school roll of 534 students — so, about 10%; but the active school roll was about 460. About 80 students had not been seen for months or years, in some cases. 'But Cathy,' I said in exasperation to the other EWO, 'we need to prosecute the parents.' ' Oh, but you don't want Darren here,' she said in alarm, about the particular student we were discussing. 'He's huge. He looks like an adult. He's been driving a car round here for ages.'

It will take a day to prepare the evidence for a court hearing, and we are trying to take about ten families to court at any one time. We started to think of more productive ways of using the EWO's skills and time. One of these was to set up a partnership with the local fire service for a sustained training course aimed at poor attenders. The EWO would be our attached member of staff, working alongside the fire officers.

Behind those deeply troubled young boys there was a dark hinterland. Since leaving the school I have sat in others where students are excluded for not wearing the correct uniform; for swearing. We dealt with huge problems in such a matter of fact way that we did not exclude students who would have been cast out of other schools. You can become highly skilled in managing and containing such students together, so that you only exclude the most extreme.

For many of them, what they meet in school is exactly the same as what exists in their community, but with a singular difference: in school, there is order; most of the adults have a real liking and respect for them; they are treated as individuals with worthwhile hopes for the future. What they learn is, on the whole, positive. But if there are too many troubled young people together in school as well as out of it, they begin to believe that life is like that for everyone. School simply reinforces the same message: they are the outcasts. As we excluded one boy he wept bitterly, saying, 'I've been excluded from the worst school in the county.'

Managing disruption

My early assurance to staff that their relationships with students were fundamental to the success of the school was amply rewarded in what I saw, time after time, in the way they showed students how to behave.

Here is a corridor scene. I am on patrol, walkie-talkie in hand, bearing down on the hefty Gavin kicking a fellow Year 8 student half his size. The year head gets there just as I am about to let rip. 'OK, Gavin?' putting his hand on Gavin's shoulder. Gavin always looked depressed but aggressive. 'Are you in class with me now? Who's been bullying you?' I watch Gavin's shoulders drop and all the aggression drain away. He walks quietly away with his teacher, ready to apologize and to go into class.

Here's another view, of me nose to nose with one of the most difficult of boys. Following an exclusion, he is supposed to be attending the Alternative Centre for Education every morning; but instead he turns up here, wrecking an Art lesson and refusing to leave the corridor area. I try to persuade him to come away with me, but I have no credibility with him. We employ an ex-policeman on patrol too, and he arrives at this point. I suddenly sense that he wants to remove Leo by force. I say, 'Leo, you need to go to ACE; but come with me to my study for bit so we can talk about it. You know that I am not going to use physical force on you, don't you? No one in the school will use physical force.'

Boy and ex-policeman look at one another intently. The boy is not going to leave of his own volition now that the adult, who would have probably used some strength of arm to eject him, cannot do so. We share the dilemma. I know that a face-saving way out of the situation is urgently needed, and if nothing presents itself the boy will use his fists. Suddenly one of the other longstanding staff appears, on his way to teach. 'Leo,' he says, putting an arm round the boy's shoulder, 'how are you? Haven't seen you for a bit. Come with me.' The two walk quietly away.

A superb teacher comes to me in a rage one morning, just to talk himself into knowing how to handle something. 'Larry has just wrecked my lesson with the Year 10s.' Larry is another of the intelligent marauders in Year 11. Exceptionally quick-witted, with long-standing disillusion about school, and cultivated habits of disruption, he regularly makes lessons unteachable by the best of teachers.

On this occasion, he has written foul abuse across the whiteboard in permanent ink. The teacher has had to teach the lesson with bright-coloured abuse behind him. 'I am so angry with him, he's just done really good work for me, and I don't understand why he has to do this.' Yet again, I watch an adult man swallow his anger and think about a constructive way forward. Larry is sent for, and comes. Part of the punishment involves this female principal standing by whilst he is invited to agree that his behaviour was unacceptable. His teacher carefully explains that he could have shouted and behaved in a typical male fashion, but he does not believe this would be right. He wants Larry to apologize and then to spend lunchtime in cleaning off the abuse.

The removal fluid is exceedingly unpleasant to handle and it is hard to get even the faintest of marks off. It takes an hour of scrubbing at the board. Larry quietly gets on with it. He has been shown how mature men behave and in his heart he wants to be the same.

We have made space in the school for such encounters. They matter as much as anything conveyed in a formal lesson. Each meeting helps to make the school more secure, more emotionally stable.

Chapter 7

Term 4: Spring 2002

In January 2002, our Inspector brought two other colleagues to the school, each of them specializing in a different area. He wanted to be certain that if he brought the school out of Special Measures it would not be into yet another category. We needed a clean bill of health, not something provisional.

When he told us that he was happy to declare the school no longer in Special Measures, I automatically threw back my head and said, 'Thank you God.' Afterwards, Kathy Stonier said that she thought our Inspector felt very emotional. She was sure there were tears in his eyes.

None of us felt jubilant; there was just the sense that now we could get on with it ourselves, without the continual outside monitoring which suggests a parent — child relationship. We knew that this was the beginning of the real process of becoming secure. What we all knew had been confirmed: the school was still immensely fragile. Our Inspector was concerned about the multiplicity of complex problems we had to manage, especially in relation to the other schools in the city. It was as if there were two schools, he thought: the students who attended, and those who did not.

I thought another statistic was relevant here, too: called the Pareto Principle, it points out how often generalizations seem to fit the ratio of 80:20. It was really hard to shift the attendance figure above 80%; 20% of students tended not to come to school however hard we worked. There was another 80-20 ratio concealed within the 80% attendance statistic. Only 20% of these students had levels of measurable ability (in conventional terms) that could be called 'average or above'. The rest had difficulties ranging from the mild to the profound. There are commonly taken tests of ability called 'the cognitive abilities tests scores' or CATS. Possible scores range from 1 to 9; 9 is exceptionally high, and 5, therefore, is the average. In other words, in a comprehensive school you would expect the average CAT score of students to be 5; but at the College of Media Arts, the average score was 3.7.

Life after Special Measures

I felt that my mission in earnest started now: to represent these troubled children, to make sure that their life chances would be the same as those from 'successful' families.

I rang the journalists who had called me about the school's being bottom of the Attendance Tables. 'We're out of Special Measures.' 'Oh, really?' I left messages — please tell X to call me. No one did and I sensed the scale of what was ahead. This was what I knew from my independent school days. Parents do not necessarily choose schools for their real qualities but for what they perceive. Those perceptions can be traced to their own schooldays, or to extraordinarily trivial issues (are their socks pulled up? I knew an experienced headteacher who chose a primary school for his son because the socks were *not* pulled up. He did not want his son to be forced to conform in trivial ways.)

The Director of Education came into every classroom of the school to congratulate the students and I was touched by the time he spent on it. We could see what it meant to those whose only memory was of being at a school in Special Measures — which included those in Year 11; that was how long the school had been deemed a failure.

Shortly afterwards I learned unofficially from the Admissions Office that only 37 students from Year 6 in primary schools had chosen the school when the school needed at least 120, and had spaces for them. For the first time I wanted to keep information away from the staff. They had only just discovered that they were officially 'making good progress'.

Suddenly the pressures of the PFI were reasserted in an acute form.

When the City Council had decided in 1999 that its new Fresh Start school would be included in the PFI contract, there had been about 650 students on roll, and at one time there had been about 1200. When I was discussing student numbers, before taking up the post of principal, numbers had already dropped to about 530; and because of my experience in the independent sector I was acutely aware of the enormous difficulty of increasing the numbers again, even if the school were to be academically successful — there is all too much evidence from the independent sector that good academic results do not in themselves keep a school viable. In December 2000 I was assured there would be 120 students in Year 7 for the following September. There were about 80. I projected the numbers through their life in the school, in the sort of budget exercise I had taken for granted in my former headships. In my conversations with the Assistant Director responsible for PFI, I struggled with the astonishing fact that the LEA had included the school in the PFI on the assumption that there would be about 180 students entering the school every year. They, not the school, controlled the admissions. How was this number to be achieved?

After many a negotiation we achieved a compromise: that in five years time there would be about 700 students and for this we needed 120 students for September 2002, and 150 for every following year. It was not just our viability in question, but the PFI costs. Whether or not the students were on the school roll, we would have to start paying Jarvis as if they were because that was how the contract was drawn.

The LEA's administration of its admissions policy, and the decisions it made, gave us great financial problems.

Adverse effects of coming out of Special Measures

Whilst schools are in Special Measures they are protected in a few ways. Staff can be required to meet for longer than in other schools (60 minutes a week is the recommendation of teacher unions in an ordinary school, regardless of whether that meeting is for training and development or counting shoes.) Schools are able to refuse to accept students from the Admissions authority that they think will adversely affect the school.

Once out of Special Measures, all concessions are abandoned.

Staff training and development: 'meetings'

My first bruising encounter with this loss of concessions was an encounter with staff who were local union representatives, who very politely and cheerfully explained that now the school was out of Special Measures they no longer had to come to all these meetings. What meetings? I organized no meetings for administration at all. In fact, there were no meetings I could recognize apart from daily briefings.

Throughout the previous year, one of our major strategies for bringing the school out of Special Measures was to create a substantial training and development time every week. We needed new ways of doing things; the training was intended to be incremental so that staff could try something out in class and then bring it to colleagues for advice. Headteachers are able to direct the time of teachers for 1265 hours each year; we included the training time in that quota, but it made no difference.

But the unions say we must not do this now: only 60 minutes per week.

I talked to national union officials who were sympathetic but referred me to the local area agreements. I could not require staff to attend meetings for more than one hour per week; 'It isn't a meeting, it's training,' I said. It did not matter. Everything would be counted as a meeting.

I could not imagine such a situation in an independent school. Everyone would have understood at the most basic level that their salaries depended on the viability of the school. In practice, I had found staff willing to work well beyond what was reasonable and had sometimes to pull them back, in case they became exhausted.

It was several months before I discovered that the local union representatives had not consulted their colleagues in the staffroom. The overwhelming majority of staff would have continued to come to training sessions because they wanted them.

Finding normality

What we now had to do was plan for normal life — which meant planning for a further reduction in student numbers, at the same time as trying to finance the alternative strategies for helping students to succeed.

A small group of us were spending hours on redesigning the curriculum again, for this shrinking school — trying at the same time to focus on the potential of Media Arts. Kathy Stonier linked us to one of the further education colleges, City College, which was trying to set up a Media Technologies qualification similar to the Fine Art Foundation Year that many students enjoy. We persuaded them that if this was to be successful, there needed to be preparatory teaching in schools, starting with fourteen-year-olds. We became the partner of choice for City College.

The Media Arts group of staff planned how the school's curriculum could develop further, linking verbal and visual literacy. Already the ideas planned the previous summer by one of the working groups were in action in Year 7. Every student was learning to use a digital camera, to make and edit videos, to give critical commentary on visual images.

Another working group, at the instigation of one of our ICT technicians, was meeting Brighton and Hove Library Service. Students were to create a visual archive by taking photographs across the city of its significant buildings and its representative streets. This project arose from the Year 7 project, the aim of which was to instil a sense of pride in the students about Whitehawk as a desirable place with an intriguing history. Our aim was that they should see themselves as inhabitants of the city as a whole, not just Whitehawk, able to contribute to the well-being of the city; and to find rewarding and interesting work there, too.

The alternative curriculum: Lifeskills

With our adviser from the EAZ we were making concrete plans for the alternative curriculum. The current initiative was not wholly successful, but there had been real improvements in attendance and attitude from some students. We were on the right lines. Now we needed the permanent structure.

Schools had been given money to appoint someone responsible for Social Inclusion; in our school, as in many, this had been taken to mean focusing on how to manage students with emotional and behavioural difficulties, usually through working with small numbers. This funding would eventually be withdrawn.

I felt that the most 'socially inclusive' activity we could provide would be through the curriculum rather than trying to remedy bad experiences, which could take a lifetime. Every time students were withdrawn from class for 'support' they picked up the notion that they were not coping. I wanted them to experience doing well.

We decided to set up a separate unit, called Lifeskills, which would be managed by the Social Inclusion Manager. Instead of working with just a few students she would have charge of all those students in Years 10 and 11 who would be following a flexible curriculum.

At the same time, we would appoint alongside her someone whose main role would be to find and make opportunities right across the curriculum and the city for learning about the rewards of employment. In this idea, I was drawing on my independent school experience that the importance of the formal, classroom curriculum is overstated. Some of the most invigorating learning comes almost by accident. I thought we should plan, rather than relying on serendipity. One example might be making contact with the archivist at Bodiam Castle when the standard History trip was planned, so that the students did not just learn about materials on their History course, but about the day-to-day work possibilities of employment at the Castle.

We took our proposal to New Deal for Communities, to ask if they would fund the salary of this other adult for three years and received very enthusiastic support. I described the situation in another county, where a similar unit was separate from school and beautifully equipped. If this programme worked, they urged me to put in another bid in two or three years for just such a separate unit.

Visual intelligence revisited: a new approach to literacy

On another front, I was finding the doubtful benefits of teaching English to a Year 9 class, and coming to terms with the sheer awfulness of Key Stage 3 tests viewed by English teachers who love teaching. The materials I was expected to teach incensed me — both the way in which Shakespeare was to be taught as a set text, rather than as living drama, and the exclusive nature of much of what was provided. In the independent sector I had been used to scrutinizing all assessments to make sure they were not divisive — for instance, explaining who Guy Fawkes was if we were asking children to respond to a story about November 5. There was little of such sensitivity in the National Curriculum tests.

We did not use National Curriculum tests in the independent schools that I led because I had been advised that they would interfere with learning. Now I could see for myself why those teachers were right. I would not have expected able academics to sit through Key Stage 3 English: they would have found it difficult, boring and condescending. In my class there were 26 students, 18 of whom were on the school's SEN register. I was determined to teach and not to occupy them. The 'Literacy Strategy' we were compelled to follow seemed to me an anti-literacy strategy.

Every time I met someone from the Standards and Effectiveness Unit of the DfES I lobbied for the right to be creative with the curriculum. I wanted to exempt the students from the standard end of Year 9 tests in English, and to find more imaginative ways of teaching them, and assessing their progress. I thought the new media technologies could provide the medium. I passionately wanted to provide a curriculum that fitted the students, as I had been able to do in independent schools — if only through what was extra-curricular.

Virtual money 1

We had been told to plan for redundancies again, and had consulted some staff who, we knew, wanted to retire. Others we would not replace, but we would restructure to make space for more teaching assistants who could work alongside teachers. With at least 60% of students on the SEN register, we needed their skills. We needed all our teachers to be flexible, too, so that they would concentrate on learning rather than subjects; on the emotional factors that make learning possible rather than blocking it.

This approach would keep the maximum number in the school, as the roll shrank. Staff from other schools in the area were fearful of coming into it, such was its reputation. Teachers who stayed were seen as heroic; teachers who left needed invalid treatment in their new schools — such was the mythology I was told about by other headteachers.

Again, I struggled with the relationship between admissions and whole school viability in the circumstances where we could not control what happened. I felt that the Council was affluent, by comparison with many areas in the country, and that there must be a means of keeping funds available whilst the school found its place in the community as a whole. I asked the Chief Executive of the Council to meet me, and we had breakfast together in the Grand Hotel whilst I explained my anxieties. He had already been a sympathetic visitor to the school and seemed to understand, although he could promise nothing.

We submitted our plans to the Council and were then discomfited by a counter-proposal. It would cost the Council so much to make staff redundant that we could keep them, and the Personnel department would underwrite the increased deficit that sat in our budget. I wondered if this response had been prompted by an intervention from the Chief Executive. If so, it was well meant but unhelpful in that I was now forced into having to negotiate with the Council about replacing any member of staff at all. They wanted to monitor all appointments very strictly, in exchange for underwriting the deficit.

Staff continuity would be maintained, and I knew how important that was. Unfortunately, part of my solution had involved using the Fresh Start money to recruit additional teaching assistants. I would now be unable to do this. The governors and I decided, even so, that we probably had little alternative but to accept the LEA's proposal.

Staff who had expected redundancy sighed heavily and wondered what they would do to fill their time. We had already designed a curriculum without them.

I reflected on the hours and hours of time we had spent in planning and negotiating in the last six or seven months. The option of rejecting the LEA's proposals did not really exist, because maintained schools are reliant on more than goodwill. The LEA always has the right to take control of a school's budget, or to refuse to indemnify a decision.

Our options were further narrowed because we had accepted the PFI proposals, even though it was clear that we would lose yet more control over decisions and actions. There would be no other resources for redeveloping the school as a physically coherent institution. The other three schools had voted for Jarvis as their preferred bidder and the LEA advisory team had decided that the Jarvis bid offered best value for money.

We braced ourselves for the arrival of Jarvis on site in the summer term, to prepare for building.

Chapter 8

Term 5: Summer 2002

Moving house: preparing for PFI

I had been involved in a major project at Wimbledon, where building a brand new junior school involved demolishing classrooms used by the secondary school pupils as well as rehousing the entire junior school in temporary classrooms. We had spent many, many hours planning the complex moves that would be required and I had been deeply involved. But I knew that I could not afford to be distracted by talk about furniture, rotas, regulations or the size of new rooms, however important to our future, at the College of Media Arts. Nothing should distract me from my main role of developing the educational stability and richness of the school.

I delegated to one of leadership team the task of managing the educational impact of having builders on the premises. His target was just that: to ensure that there were no adverse effects on student learning. We were not just having a new building, but a comprehensive redesign of classrooms and corridors, to try to make the maze into a building with a heart.

He spent his hours negotiating with staff and the site manager about the sequence of packing and removal: which rooms would be closed down, in which order; which corridors would be blocked, which lavatories would remain in use and how access to these was to be achieved; how to get in and out of the school without crossing into territory now required by builders. It was like trying to predict the sequence for giving order to a Rubik cube — but fraught with feelings that had to be managed.

Gradually, throughout the term, whole classrooms were packed away, temporary accommodation was inhabited and corridors were blocked off. It began to feel dangerous to me. Even the safest of schools has to be careful when builders are in; bringing the builders into this most fragile of schools was like introducing a toddler to a house of cards.

Virtual money 2

One day the Bursar called me in some perplexity. Our outline budget had been returned from the LEA with a huge deficit.

I rang the Finance Office of the Council to speak to the former Chair of the Governors' Finance Committee, who had just resigned because of major restructuring in the Council (see p110). We missed his advice. I asked him about the deficit. What had happened to the LEA's promise to put the saved redundancy money into our budget?

'Well, yes,' he said. 'I kept telling the personnel department that they couldn't promise to offset your deficit. They don't have the budget to do it.'

This had to be explained to me very carefully. Although the personnel department would have funds to make staff redundant, it did not hold a budget for this purpose. No one holds a budget for making people redundant. Money is found, in the miraculous way that happens, from somewhere in the Council budget: a virement (or freedom to vary how budgeted money is to be spent) that in this case worked against us.

So the deficit was to sit in the school's budget, making our situation look ever more precarious. I rang the Assistant Director for School Improvement who had brokered the idea. 'Ah,' she said thoughtfully. 'So what is it, then? Virtual money?' We ruminated together.

Then I went back to the task of trying to find essential work for the highly paid teachers who were still on the staff instead of having been made redundant. I longed for ways of escaping this ludicrous situation.

Partnerships

The outsiders who were happiest about the school's coming out of Special Measures were the Diocese of Chichester and United Learning Trust. Both wanted to help us; both felt it would be easier if the school had already demonstrated that it could run like a 'normal' school. In theory we were now freer to make our own decisions. Although the LEA would have to put together another action plan to support the school, it would be much smaller.

Faith School initiative

I met the Diocesan Director of Education several times; and talked to the governors about what might be possible. Reactions varied from the downright suspicious to the highly enthused. They needed more information. A small number representing the school, the Diocese and the LEA met on a number of occasions and by May 2002 had produced a preliminary briefing paper, together with suggestions for the school and the Diocese to form a partnership. The most exciting aspect, I thought, was that Lord Dearing agreed to chair the first meeting of a wider representative group. His report on Church of England secondary schools gave him enormous authority and experience on which to draw.

One of the teacher governors, an agnostic, came out of the meeting fully convinced of the value of the partnership. Derek Bown, confirmed atheist, had always been in favour. He regularly said he would sell his soul to the devil to get the school fully established and successful. What pleased me most was the response of those who came from Hove: Hove with its reputation for looking down on Brighton; its conviction that good breeding resided in its streets. Representatives from Hove were overwhelmingly supportive, and one commented quietly that our biggest problem would be the LEA, because of the political background. I did not fully understand this, but took her word about it.

The Bishop started looking for a suitable chaplain to the school. There would be suspicion in the community that could only be broken by personal experience with the new chaplain.

Academy progress

For many months nothing happened and I thought nothing would. I had started looking towards the New Deal for Communities, especially because there was a very successful club for children and young people from the estate called the Crew Club. Lorraine, a former teaching assistant, and her partner Darren had selflessly set this up. At first, their home was just open at all times so that school absconders could have a safe place. Then they took over an old building on the estate and smartened it up, instituting rules for behaviour and planning ahead. They put an ambitious suggestion to New Deal for a completely new building with some classrooms as well as other facilities. It was a proposal for 'not school'.

I could see what they wanted and could only applaud their intentions, but I saw it as potentially subversive. We had an increasingly empty school on which money was being spent. Could we not work together?

But as months went by, and I saw how deeply prejudiced parents were about the school — the proposed number of entrants for September 2002 was still dismally small — I no longer thought of the school as for the immediate local community. I did not see how it would benefit the students to confirm their narrowness of experience. And then, in July 2002, Angela Rumbold rang to say ULT had found a sponsor for the school: 'He knows you. He doesn't want to be known at the moment,' and then she told me who it was.

By the end of the Summer of 2002 I had told the Fresh Start

unit as well as the senior leadership team about the idea that the school could become independent, as an Academy, with a faith partnership with the Diocese of Chichester which would encourage students of all faith backgrounds to apply; and it would be, first and foremost, for the marginalized children of East Brighton. They could be *chosen*, for once, instead of being rejected.

Admissions: you take the students we send

We were having to admit more and more dysfunctional students, some of whom had 'requested' a transfer to the school from one of the other Brighton and Hove schools. At admissions meetings with College of Media Arts staff, parents would freely tell us that they had removed their child from another school under the threat that, otherwise, 'we may have to enforce a permanent exclusion'.

Scarcely had we begun to settle and stabilize the large number of distressed and dysfunctional students than more arrived from other schools. Families being rehoused from violent situations elsewhere, for instance, in London, would present themselves. As we began to make marginal improvements to attendance we were directed to take a few students who had not been in school for months.

I consulted Anthony Edkins, headteacher of Falmer High School, for advice. He had been highly successful in appealing to the Secretary of State to overrule a enforced admission. He had been canny in manipulating the Bromcom system. I also consulted one of the primary school heads who had made marked improvements in his school's attendance.

We needed to analyse all our data in detail to see if we could find evidence that these admissions were damaging. I consulted the Code of Practice for Admissions, and found the paragraph stating that that LEAs did not have to direct difficult students to schools with unusually high proportions of very challenging students, or which had recently come out of Special Measures.

Our Education Welfare Officer embarked on serious analysis of data. He spent several weeks looking at where students who transferred in mid-year came from, their previous attendance records, their levels of literacy, their behaviour. He identified the impact of their poor attendance and achievement on our average statistics. I wanted to appeal to the Authority under the Code of Practice for Admissions not to send us such students: as if a troupe of acrobats, having achieved their balancing act, had to accommodate without reason or notice a series of uncoordinated learners who unbalanced everyone again.

I presented the information to governors at the end of the Summer Term and was asked to send it to the Director of Education (or Children, Families and Schools — CFS as it was now known) on their behalf. This, at least, was heartening. Governors fully understood and wanted to campaign too.

The end of the Summer Term 2002 found me very weary, now: exhilarated by what the students were actively achieving; struggling with the forces of inertia or reaction that were internal as well as external.

I was trying to persuade those staff who were not taking up their roles fully, to leave. I knew from Kathy Stonier that the rest of the staff were delighted. They would never say so in public. You have to put up with being seen to be harsh by a few who complain loudly, whilst the quiet majority rejoice because justice is being upheld.

But the governors were fully supportive, there was a lot of goodwill from students; and plans afoot: affiliation to the Diocese of Chichester; becoming an Academy.

No one outside the school really understood the complexity of what was achieved by the end of this term, or of the growing sense of strength and security among students. Two incidents in particular exemplified this: one was the long assembly already described; the other was the glorious occasion when we achieved a happy coincidence of good behaviour and good food. During the World Cup, we needed to be sure that GCSE candidates — in fact, any students at all — would come to school for their examinations. So we organized a large screen and data projector in the dining room, talked sweetly to the chief cook (Flo had considerable charisma and we had to fight to keep her) and the dining room filled up with staff and students, eating rolls filled with bacon or sausages and cheering on the England side to victory. A number of colleague heads and senior staff from other schools were in the school that morning and I invited them to have breakfast too. They were profoundly impressed by the way in which staff 'framed' the desired behaviour for the students and the truly warm and disciplined relationships that obviously existed between staff and students.

But there was PFI.

Chapter 9

Term 6: Autumn 2002

Opening late: the real impact of Jarvis

The Autumn term did not start well. Jarvis had mismanaged the work of the summer holidays and we had to start nine days late, having had no access to any of the school during the holidays. I had no study as yet.

Equally difficult was knowing that the few new Year 7 students who we knew intended to come might drift away because of the late start. We had to keep our nerve. Day One for new entrants was filled with rumour. 'Well, Phil,' to the head of Year 7, 'how many turned up? I only counted about 50.' 'Ah no, I saw about 60. It's better than you think.' Hardly.

The health of the school depends on the capacity of its leaders to assimilate and make sense of the school's experiences. In the Autumn Term of 2002 I began to experience what the people of Whitehawk must have seen so often that they became inured to it.

When organizations change, what happens to those for whom they are responsible? And if schools are so intertwined with their communities, how are the changes in society at large to be managed so that schools are not just caught in the backwash? I began to experience for myself the pressure to make and keep the school almost invisible — the scapegoat for the rest of the city: the innocent one who is cast out into the desert to carry society's sins. At the time, it felt like 'death by a thousand cuts', which was how I referred to it — a bleeding away of what gives us colour, energy and life.

In hindsight, I see this bleeding away as the loss of the people who knew and understood what had happened to the school, and what ought to happen: the people with authority and commitment, who for one reason or another decided that East Brighton College of Media Arts could no longer be high in their list of priorities. This even included the DfES official running the Fresh Start unit, who moved on to another post at this time, so that I had to explain the school's history to the new civil servant.

1. The disappeared

First, there were 'the disappeared'.

Brighton and Hove Council went through a sudden transformation under its new Chief Executive. The biggest change was the merging of the LEA with Social Care, to create a new Children, Families and Schools department: a very good idea, but needing careful management. However, almost all the experienced Assistant Directors of Education vanished or changed status over a six-month period, from July to December 2002: the Assistant Director in charge of School Effectiveness, with whom I had discussed all my ideas and strategies; the Director of Schools Personnel, who understood all the difficult issues connected with staff performance or sickness; the Assistant Director in charge of both the PFI and Admissions, with whom I had politely battled about the ludicrous anomalies in predicted numbers; the Assistant Director in charge of children's services — a very perceptive man who found himself stuck with PFI and got another job by December; the manager of the PFI process, who had accompanied our tussles to get sensible plans from Jarvis.

Another loss (already mentioned) was the chair of the school's Finance Committee (see p103), who had resigned because the restructuring of the Council was overwhelming in its demand on his time.

When these people disappeared they took with them a corporate understanding of the pressures and realities with which we lived, and the strategies we had adopted to steer our way through. We had shared experiences, stories, and understanding. Now I had to start again.

2. The promoted

Where good professional development for teachers is encouraged in a school you have to expect them to get promotions. Professionally alert schools normally recruit new staff very easily. We were developing this culture at the College of Media Arts: several teaching assistants wanted to qualify as teachers, either through the Graduate Teacher Recruitment Programme or through other kinds of certification. But we only had limited reserves to support would-be teachers. We needed experts with deep experience, maturity and sheer expertise.

With a mixture of pleasure and horror, therefore, I found myself congratulating: first, an assistant principal who was promoted to the post of deputy head in a very secure school; then another assistant principal who had decided on a complete change of life, away from education, to fulfil a long-held dream; then the vice principal, Kathy Stonier, who gained her first headship at a stable and well-regarded school nearby. It was thoroughly well-deserved; but replacing them would be very hard. Another traveller at this point was the clerk to the governors. As former principal of a local sixth form college he was very knowledgeable. He was fulfilling a dream, too — a year travelling in the Far East. He had been saving for years for this. Two of these people left at the end of the Summer Term 2002 and the others would leave at the end of the Autumn Term.

With these colleagues I had spent a lot of time, built up trust and ways of working. In most schools, such changes are easily assimilated. There was a group of staff inside the school I had identified as the future extended leadership team and I knew they had abundant skills to offer; but from May 2002 I started to pick up, one after another, the responsibilities that the staff who were leaving had held. I would not keep these roles for ever; once I had completed the process of coaching other staff they would feel confident about taking on new responsibilities.

However, we had spent most of our energy in getting out of Special Measures, learning to be accountable to ourselves again, and preparing for PFI. Coaching and developing staff is a long-term process. In the meantime, then, I took responsibility for attendance, for inclusion (which meant in reality exclusions), for the operational detail of the PFI — all huge areas requiring highly detailed understanding and involvement.

Attendance and inclusion fell to me because we could not afford to replace the assistant principal who had been in charge; or, if we had done so, we would have been penalized by the finance department of the LEA. I took charge of the detail of the PFI because continuity would be needed once the assistant principal to whom I had allocated it had left. But I was fearful and angry about this diversion from my central role. I resented having to be so closely involved. *Jarvis:* 'We need regular meetings.' *Me:* 'How often?' *Jarvis:* 'We probably need about four hours every week.' *Director of Children, Families and Schools:* 'The other heads don't seem to have a problem. You could just set aside an afternoon every week.' I refused to start the meetings before 4 PM. At least I could devote the school day to the school.

Increasing workload

Since the school came out of Special Measures in January 2002, I had started work at home by 6 am; been at my desk in school soon after half-past seven, and carried on without intermission for the next twelve hours. Home was just the other part of the office. Weekends and holidays passed in a blur of more work. It had never mattered before, but now it did.

The greatest loss was Kathy Stonier, the vice principal. Although her new post would not begin until January 2003, I encouraged her to visit her new school as often as needed. GDST had made it possible for me to visit College of Media Arts several times whilst I was still running Wimbledon High School. I thought Kathy deserved the same opportunities.

I had loved working with Kathy. We had laughed a lot. But now the fun seemed to have evaporated under the stress of the workload.

3. The sick

Those were the permanent losses; there were other kinds of disappearance, which were almost as intractably difficult to handle. Ever since I had joined the school I had met long-standing sickness among staff of a kind I had never before experienced. It was another indication of the school's fragility. One of the assistant principals said he thought the building was sick.

In my two years there was never a Head of English; we were quite unable to recruit anyone. The teacher who had acted as Head of English, who was actually in charge of Literacy (highly significant in a school where so many struggled to read) was herself off sick for more of the time than she was present. We did briefly engage a lovely teacher as Head of English but within six weeks of starting in September 2002 he too fell ill.

The Special Educational Needs Coordinator — another vital role in a school where at least 60% were on the register of Special Needs — struggled with recurrent health problems, and was often absent for weeks on end.

The educational psychologist we had recruited to work for 50% of her time in the school did not come into school at all in the autumn of 2002. She too was ill.

Other areas of the school were bursting with energy and forward thinking; but in the areas where we needed most skill, most sustained effort and concentration, we had fewest resources. No one seemed to be available from the advisory service to stand in. Advisers were willing to give advice, but not to teach. We wanted teachers.

The lack of our educational psychologist was damaging because of her understanding of the real situation in the school.

Through her status in the Educational Psychology Service for Brighton and Hove, we had objective representation at Council level. She said she could easily write statements of special educational need for at least 20% of the students; that the biggest problems were of mental health, strongly affected by domestic violence. Parents, she said, seemed to brush aside the matter of domestic violence. They did not see the relationship between this and disturbed behaviour in adolescence.

She knew of a radical Canadian programme for integrating teaching and the emotional curriculum, and we had devised a new approach that would place her in the classroom for some of the time, alongside mainstream teachers. We needed an educational psychologist to help us transform our ways of working; and she had creative ideas.

The Chief Educational Psychologist and I had met on a regular basis. He was new to Brighton and was trying to understand the situation. As we talked he recalled this fable.

'Do you know the story of the crocodile hunter? There was a town at the bottom of which was a deep swamp. And every year in the hot weather the crocodiles crawled out of it and climbed up the hill. So the residents hired a crocodile hunter to kill the crocodiles before they could get up the hill. But what they should have done was clear the swamp.'

4. Building a new team

Despite all these losses, I wanted to build on the existing levels of skill in the staff. I knew that being out of Special Measures meant becoming strong through our internal systems. There was now only one other member of the leadership team fully engaged in the work of the school; he was a wonderful teacher and a tough, challenging thinker. We had several other equally skilled staff, gradually discovering how to be comfortable with responsibility at this level.

In a different school, I would have been excited instead of troubled. But the long-standing staff had needed much coaxing to take on new experiences. Their first instinct was still to retreat and to remember things going wrong in the past. New staff saw this and became anxious too. Victim mentality is infectious, I found.

Recruiting a Consultant Head

We would not be able to recruit a new vice principal until April 2003. I also hoped that if the school were to become an Academy we would attract interesting applicants. We needed someone of Consultant Leader status for a term or two to work in the school — someone to whom I would not have to explain the pitfalls, and who could help coach others.

I rang someone at the Fresh Start unit. To my relief he knew just the person. She had recently been part of a new Trainee Head programme, and was willing to join the school for two terms.

Coping with the Council Admissions

Apart from making sense of PFI, I suddenly remembered my unanswered letter about having so many challenging students allocated to us. As a proportion of the new, small intake, they were greater than ever. The cocktail of dysfunctional personalities was ever more dangerous. The Assistant Director now in charge of PFI looked at me wearily. 'You haven't had an answer? When did you write?' 'July.' It was now September. 'I'll get you a response.' When it came, the letter was standard fare from the Admissions Department: other schools coped so we should, too.

Conversations with the new department of Children, Families and Schools acquired a bizarre unreality. I was summoned to a meeting with representatives of unions, advisors, directors, and decided to take with me the assistant principal in charge of the curriculum. He managed the staffing too. He was passionate, totally in command of his material, and impartial; it would be good experience for him and supportive to me.

This meeting suddenly became an inquisition from the Director of Children, Families and Schools about 'low staff morale':

Why were so many staff leaving? I could not say openly that they had taken the money without doing the job properly; that the personnel department had formally endorsed everything; that other staff were quietly cheering. These were confidential matters.

I described instead the practice of 'trade' which I had brought with me from Wimbledon High School. I was always happy for someone to take time off 'for a friend's wedding' or 'to see Ben playing Joseph in the Nativity Play' because I knew that they would repay the time in triplicate. We monitored this carefully to make sure that no one exploited their freedom. 'Do you really do that?' asked the regional officer from the NUT. 'Well, I think that's wonderful.'

'What about your reduced curriculum? Do you have a curriculum plan?' The link advisor felt moved to intervene. 'Well, of course — the College has had to have plans for HMI.' Curriculum balance, appropriateness and innovation were my passion and my starting point — even when making staff redundant.

I left the meeting feeling baffled. Something very odd was happening. I was completely unused to having my educational judgement questioned in this way. I suddenly felt that I would not have been believed had not someone else from my team been present.

Academy hopes confirmed

However, there was good news too. The Chief Executive of United Learning Trust had arranged a meeting for me, Derek Bown, the proposed sponsor and Angela Rumbold at Lambeth Palace.

Afterwards, Derek and I stood at the bar on Victoria Station, overlooking the concourse whilst we drank wine and felt euphoric beyond description. It had been a wonderful meeting; the sponsor had listened gravely whilst I described what I planned for the school and then, halfway through, said, 'The two million will be all right.' Originally he had promised a quarter of a million pounds of the two million needed.

His only stipulation was absolute anonymity for himself.

ULT's only stipulation was that the school could not stay in the PFI. The Chief Executive would try to extricate it. He had visited the school and seen what was being done. It fell so far short of his standards that he could not accept the work. He thought that the school might need to be razed to the ground so that a sensible building could be erected. I thought he was right. He prepared to talk to the Secretary of State for Education.

Parallel plans: Federation

The Director of CFS was clearly troubled by the rising deficit and the failure to divert pupils to the school. I was still not free to talk to him about the Academy proposals, which would, I hoped, bring great relief. In the meantime, he thought we should consider the implications of the new legislation which would make Federation possible: in his proposal, our working together with Varndean, the local Beacon school.

There were several ways in which a federation could work: schools could voluntarily work together developing common practices and ideas; or one school could take the lead to support another; or the governing bodies could become one entity; or one set of senior staff and governors could completely take over the leadership and management of another, weaker, school.

I thought it would be a good idea to explore if the Academy proposal came to nothing because it would associate the school everyone loathed with one they admired and could provide another way of breaking down prejudice. Many middle-class parents would be horrified at the idea of their children being in class with children from Whitehawk, but I knew they needed to be shocked into recognition of the intelligence and rights of Whitehawk children. I was invited to devise some ways of joint working, and set my mind to it; but it was utterly confidential to me and the Head of Varndean, our two chairs of governors, and the Director.

Many people knew about the proposed link with the Diocese; the management team knew about the Academy because I did not want them to feel distrusted. But I said nothing about the Federation. I was very disconcerted, a few weeks later, to find how many people in the LEA were aware of the idea of the Federation. We had been enjoined to secrecy. But apparently this was relative.

In the meantime the tasks mounted.

The story of the PFI: Jarvis

Jarvis contractors were busily tearing the heart out of the school. In an effort to create an enlarged and coherent corridor structure, branching from the main highway that they wanted to call 'The Street', they drove a wedge into the school which divided it from itself.

At the same time as coping with the ever-extending list of complaints from staff about missing equipment, cold and leaking rooms, new facilities without the expected specifications, I trawled through the small print of the documentation to see the discrepancies between what we thought we were getting and what was eventually arriving. It seemed that 'slimming down the budget' was a skill this contractor had refined wonderfully; and it was only to be discovered by extreme attention to detail. I found myself defending the school's position on innumerable occasions.

An illustration of what tended to happen is found in the saga of the radio station.

Having had superb experience of a pupil-run school radio station at The Royal Naval School, I desperately wanted one for these students. I wanted their parents to hear them on air and articulate, as I was sure they would be. This is one of the most potent forms of Student Voice that I know.

I researched radio licences and masts, costs of software and performing rights, made contact with local enthusiasts and convinced New Deal for Communities to promise funding because the community would use the radio station too. BBC Southern Counties donated the equipment and American Express in Brighton provided money for furniture.

But then there was Jarvis.

Right from the start I told the architects that the new media arts building would have to make space for a radio station. The room would be small, but the main costs would be for trunking for cabling, power and the like, if necessary to allow us to introduce television in the future. I wanted to make the building as flexible and adaptable as possible, knowing how fast the media technology develops. I recognized that Jarvis had made no provision for such costs in their design and asked for estimates, because New Deal would pay the difference.

The architect seemed happy enough; but there ensued a long silence. After many unanswered emails I rang him. He was highly embarrassed. Someone in the Jarvis hierarchy had told him to stop talking to me. I said, 'But we are being given a radio station. It needs to go into the new block. We will be placing it there once the building is ready.' I could almost hear his shoulder-shrug and had a premonition of what would happen.

From Jarvis: 'There was no radio station in the specification. Why are you introducing this at the last minute? Didn't you realize that there will be significant cost implications?'

Everyone at Jarvis whom I had met for detailed discussions seemed to have vanished. There was no one willing to accept that all of this had been long ago anticipated.

I had no energy for this fight because there were so many others. For instance, Jarvis had made no bid to renovate the truly dreadful science laboratories, with thirty-year-old graffiti on benches, blackout and blinds in tatters, and unreliable gas and water supplies. We persuaded the Fresh Start Unit to make us a capital grant.

The refurbishment coincided with the arrival on site of Jarvis, who had said they would have nothing to do with renovating the science laboratories. Good, we said. We could watch the budget and make sure nothing was wasted.

Ah, but no contractor other than one approved by Jarvis could enter the site. Snag. Jarvis declared that they would run the contract. Our chosen contractors had to work their way past the site manager, whose reliability was by then much in doubt.

We were going through recurring cycles of frustration: being asked for information — position of doors and windows, location of network points and so on — providing maps and lists, only to have their existence denied. No, he had not received the information. After the summer holidays of 2002, when the school staff had no access to any part of the school for six weeks, a great deal of school equipment disappeared. School staff must be dreadfully careless, we were told.

The budget for the renovation of the laboratories, which had contained enough to supply interactive whiteboards and other facilities, suddenly ran dry. There were drains that had to be completely replaced; different levels of power we had not thought about; and so on. The site manager looked at us pityingly as he explained what a favour Jarvis had done in sorting out all the problems of refurbishing science on our behalf. Look how insufficient our budget would have been for the task.

We said: but if you had surveyed the site properly in the first place you would have known about the state of the drains; just as you would have located our Internet link which you neatly severed one afternoon, claiming to have no mention of the link on any maps. If you had seen how awful the drains were, how unfit for purpose the laboratories, you would have included these in the specifications for a refit. You are about to take over responsibility for the fabric of the building for the next twenty-five years.

The lower corridor, from which almost all stairways branched out into the different areas of the school, was inaccessible. The front entrance of the school led nowhere. To reach the main hall, students had to cross through the narrow reception area having first come through other classrooms. The alternative was to cross a raised temporary walkway that was slippery and wide open to the winds and rain.

Lord Dearing came to the school for the second of our discussions with the Diocese of Chichester about becoming a partner faith school. He wanted to be shown round. Two minutes into our walk he said, perturbed, 'However can you manage this?' He instantly saw the ramifications. (He stopped for several minutes at the back of a French lesson that he also saw was excellent. We kept on with the business of education, regardless.)

Jarvis workmen had to be reminded to wear their safety helmets. They walked over the roofs without harnesses, seemingly oblivious of the role model they were offering to boys eyeing them from below.

After many months of protest on our part, the site manager was removed. Let's start again, said Jarvis management, as the project fell further and further behind, and the school still had its bizarrely dislocated form.

To make possible the reworking of the lower corridor we had organized a series of linked room closures, relocating the French department, Art, Science, ICT, Design and Technology. Contents of rooms were piled high in the main hall, in theory to be relocated before the start of the new Autumn term (2002). We turned a spare laboratory into a temporary Art room during the latter part of the summer of 2002; and returned to school to find the new Art rooms ready, but Design and Technology rooms were not. The site manager was baffled. What was the problem? 'Don't you want the new Art rooms?'

Imagine a controlled explosion in which the detonators are set off out of sequence. This was in effect our experience; and in the midst of it we had a very troubled and unsettled community with a terrible record of attendance, many temptations to play truant, and many students coming to school each day from a background of domestic chaos.

Most students were remarkably sensible. We showed them areas where we thought the safety nets were merely notional but also highly visible. We asked the students to be careful and they were. It was unimaginably harder than before to track down students who were not in class and should have been; to monitor the corners of the school. Staff on patrol could be called to an emergency and take twice as long to arrive at it as before. You could set out on a route to a classroom only to discover that you had been rerouted — doors were locked that had been open. I have the oddest moments of *déjà vue* when sitting on trains that are being rerouted round the country because of signalling problems; they have become Jarvis moments for me.

The killing combination from Jarvis was, lack of transparency, ruthless trimming of specifications to keep within an unannounced budget (we could never be certain how much was being devoted to the College of Media Arts, as opposed to the other three schools in the PFI), very poor site management, lack of sustainability in staffing, inefficiency — generally taking on far more than could realistically be managed.

We kept detailed photographic records throughout. The governors still consider that the most damaging experience the school endured was the PFI. Although Brighton and Hove Council have rebutted this there is much truth in the claim. Had Jarvis really understood what schools are about, especially in terms of the relationships to be maintained between students and staff, their entire planning process would have been utterly different. They might have looked at the school building and recognized that what was needed was a complete rebuild rather than the botched attempt to renovate from within a working environment.

I would far rather have moved everyone into a series of temporary buildings where we could have been close together, and we could have controlled the whole environment instead of having to share it with an overstretched and incoherent external organisation.

Independence under threat

However, there was an end in sight, through the Academy proposal which I was now free to discuss with the Director of CFS. He listened with guarded pleasure and began to speculate on how this could mesh with the idea of federation too. I wondered. The whole purpose of being an Academy was to escape local council control.

We gave the news to the governors, introducing them to the Chief Executive of ULT. The governors were overjoyed at the prospect of being able to govern the school independently; their questions were pointed and thorough. Staff and parent governors were sworn to keep matters to themselves and did. They were delighted beyond measure. Everyone worried about keeping the rest of the staff in the dark, but there were no alternatives until we knew we could be extracted from the PFI. Sensitivities were so acute that the only information to be given had to be accurate, with no room for rumour, speculation or anxiety.

The Diocese found a local woman priest who was deeply interested in becoming chaplain to the school. I went to visit her. She was exactly the sort of person that people would trust.

Holding on to stability

And we needed this spiritual dimension. Stresses were beginning to show where it most mattered: in Year 11. One of the most deeply buried problems in the school was sexism, and I had been dealing with it overtly for over a year because of its impact on attitudes and attendance. In the summer of 2001, one of the staff had brought an anonymous letter from a girl, which told a sorry story of repeated sexist behaviour from many of the boys in the year group. At the time they were in Year 9 and the girls wanted to get on with work. They were motivated, ambitious and sensitive. They came to tell me in person and I took the problem to the Year Head.

He had been glad for me to be involved. It was a longstanding problem. The boys would hate being addressed by a woman on the subject of their behaviour to girls. We could also bring in the Community Safety Team, to let boys know that this behaviour, if repeated, could lead to prosecution in the outside world. We wanted to change their assumption that this was how men behaved to women.

But it was likely, given some of boys concerned, that their behaviour had been learned at home. Instead of calling in the police at once, we talked to them at the start of the new academic year, to make sure they knew what we expected and judged and to set some standards. We warned them that if there were further incidents, we would tell their parents and the police.

For months no one complained and the girls became more

confident about talking to me casually. But by the summer of 2002 there were incidents too gross to overlook. The police, the parents and the boys sat down for a lengthy discussion at which the repercussions were clarified. One of the boys had been excluded twice in the meantime for his increasing harassment. But they did not really understand what sexual harassment meant — or rather, thought it was legitimate. The crisis flared up around a refugee who had joined the group — a highly intelligent Muslim girl who had come as a complete non-English speaker. The LEA's support was fairly slim: she had an hour or so each week with a specialist linguist. The rest of her support network was provided almost entirely by the same girls that had complained to me.

One day, a boy pretended to masturbate and then rubbed his hand in her face: a repellent experience for anyone but especially a Muslim. She ran home in deep distress. No adult had seen the incident, which was reported by one of the brave girls. Accusation and counter-accusation flew around the year group; very sensitive but extremely firm management would be essential.

I sought help from the Muslim community so that the refugee could explain without barriers of language or religion what had happened. One 'problem' was that she had rapidly returned to school. She was a determined girl, feeling unsafe in this country, but desperately anxious not to lose her educational opportunity. Other boys cited the fact that she was in school the next day as evidence that nothing serious had happened.

What the incident revealed was a much deeper malaise. Other girls admitted that they had similar experiences of harassment but only one was prepared to give evidence; and she was ostracized by her peers. Any girl prepared to stand up for herself (or any other girl) would be persecuted. They lived as a matter of course in a culture where such oppressive harassment was acceptable; the adults were outsiders who would be excluded. I recalled the 'sexualised estate', which health visitors had described to me.

At another bleak level, we worried now about the academic performance of the year group. Their sense of safety had disappeared, and there was a monstrous emotional turbulence to undermine their motivation.

Worse still was our fear that the boy would carry on as a sexual predator, eventually becoming a rapist. There seemed to be few social protocols for managing such issues. We could only continue to act out our own values.

There are relatively simple protocols for excluding students: for attempts to set light to someone's hair, throwing chairs, rampaging in and out of other people's classrooms. You can try to help with such behaviours because most students do not behave like this without a background of social and emotional disturbance for which you can plan. You can usually call upon advice and support from an educational psychologist and alternative educational provision, at least in part. There are no such protocols in our society for students who are becoming sexual predators; but there should be.

The beginning of the end

Suddenly everything seemed to be taken out of my hands. It began with a visit from Phil Revell, a journalist who writes for *The Times Educational Supplement, The Guardian* and other publications. Phil wanted to see what was happening now that we had been out of Special Measures for almost a year. He spent a morning in school, talking to students, walking the corridors. 'I like what I see,' he said — and this had included being confronted by one of our most troubled students. She so beguiled him that he wrote a brief piece about her quite separately. He asked about future plans. I said I could not tell him but that we were very optimistic for the future. He gave me a thoughtful look and remarked that he could make some intelligent guesses.

'The management team is jumping ship'

A week later, Phil Revell rang.

'I'm ringing to tell you that that someone in the LEA is briefing *The Times Educational Supplement* against you.' All the air vanished from my lungs. Phil was outraged. He had written his article for the *TES*, filed it, and then been told by a colleague in the news room that his article was to be killed because of another announcement going out as a news item. Three deputy heads had jumped ship; I would be leaving soon and the school would be federated with Varndean School. This was what he was told.

Phil was incredulous. I explained that what was described as 'jumping ship' was *promotion*. The senior staff referred to were angry because they had not 'jumped' anywhere — they had been promoted. They wanted to talk to him. Derek Bown had a long conversation to put the story straight for Phil's benefit, at least. Phil was angry. He felt that a good article had been quashed in favour of a manufactured news item.

I was terribly disturbed by the specific nature of the report; so few people knew about Varndean and the suggested federation that I felt bound to believe the rest of the account, too: someone was 'briefing against' me. I rang the Secondary Heads Association and was put straight through to one of its most senior officers. It was comforting to have such complete, unequivocal support.

Performance Management

Coincidentally, three of the governors were in school as I was wrestling with Phil's revelation; they had come to meet me and the External Assessor from Cambridge Educational Associates (CEA) to take me through the process of Performance Management Review — my account of the progress the school had made under my leadership in the year. I had sent a detailed report a couple of weeks previously. It was impossible to start the meeting without telling them what was happening. I was still deeply shocked. I had never met injustice in my professional life before. The governors looked at one another and then told me that one of the other governors was trying to undermine me. Two of the three governors with me were experienced educationalists. 'We felt you ought to be told about this.'

The external assessor from CEA was also an experienced professional. 'If I were in Jill's shoes I'd walk away from this now,' he said. I left that meeting knowing that they would recommend another rise in my salary. It seemed unimportant. Breathing was hard and I felt suffocated.

'The school may become an Academy'

A week or so later, the Director of the Education Action Zone alerted me to a meeting between the Director of CFS and the Head of Whitehawk Primary School (PS). She was in the process of winding down the EAZ, knew about the Academy proposals and was a very astute observer. Although I had not been invited, she thought I should be there.

One of the most important suggestions was that the Academy should eventually be an all-age school, from 4 to 16 and possible 4 to 19 but this was the first the primary headteacher had heard of the idea. He looked troubled. At one point, whilst the Director of CFS took a call on his mobile, I was able to say sotto voce, 'It's all right — your job won't be at risk.' His face cleared. That was his first worry dealt with. He was extremely anxious about the Director's intention to speak to the Whitehawk PS governors the following week.

Derek Bown and I had spent many months planning and thinking before we talked to College of Media Arts governors, when we took them carefully through a process of exploring options. They had been able to make an informed decision over a period of time. I told the Director that I would be away from my school when he was talking to Whitehawk PS governors. I was to be a facilitator at an international educational conference organized by the British Council. This had been booked many months before. I felt full of trepidation about his proposed meeting with Whitehawk PS governors.

The reality was even more disastrous than I had feared. Such had been the acrimony in the discussion that the Chair of the Council CFS group and the Director believed Whitehawk PS governors would tell the press about the Academy proposals.

They put out an announcement of their own to pre-empt it. The College of Media Arts staff heard the news on the radio as they were driving to school.

It could not have been worse. As far as they were concerned, it was yet another example of LEA duplicity and nothing that I had done in my two years at the school had made any difference to this. They perceived that this was just another example of the authority's stabbing the school in the back. 'We told you so. You can't control things in the end, whatever you say. They'll get you. Watch your back.' I was to be as powerless as anyone else who had tried to run the school.

Derek Bown and I went together into a staff meeting to try to allay fears. I explained that the Academy idea had been mine, not the Council's; that I had been working on it for about a year and a half, and that the governors were enthusiastic.

They were uncertain; suspicious. In the eyes of the staff it was as if I stood where I had two years ago: someone who would have to prove herself trustworthy. Members of the leadership team sat as far away from me as they could get. One of them asked provocative questions about the security of staff jobs and contracts. Perhaps the intention was to be devil's advocate. I was placed where I began: knowing that I was truthful, struggling in a culture of disbelief.

A few days later there was one of those typical days: several meetings clashed, my presence was essential — apparently — at all of them; there would be a very important governors' meeting in the evening, and, after much procrastination, I had an appointment in the afternoon with the Director of CFS and my SHA Field Officer to talk about the issues that had surfaced in the past weeks.

I went into the meeting feeling sceptical. It was hard not to believe he'd been the LEA officer who had briefed *The TES* against me. But it was hard, too, to understand what his purpose might have been, and he said he hadn't discussed me; perhaps it had just been loose conversation on someone's part. My Field Officer had found it extremely hard to set up any kind of meeting. The Director seemed unaware that there might be a crisis. A previous appointment she had made with him had ended as a five minute corridor discussion in the middle of another meeting. She was astonished, Normally, if she rang a Director of Education and said she wanted to talk about one of the head-teachers, 'the red carpet would be rolled out.' Not in this case.

For an hour I struggled to explain the sheer depth and detail of my work. He plainly thought I sketched out grand ideas and then floated away from them. His response to my attempt to explain the devastation of the press release, the apparently adversarial press briefing against me — the erosion of trust that had been so painstakingly built — was to say that the school could soon be back in Special Measures.

He added that the Council had agreed to a more just Admissions process, which might eventually help the school to recruit more students; but there would be no public discussion of the proposals before the local elections in May 2003, and another year of consultation before any decision would be made. There were many marginal seats and so the controlling Labour Party was afraid of provoking debate which might lose them.

My feeling of exhaustion as I left the meeting was compounded by the thought that if the future of the children was to be manipulated, yet again, by political expediency, my work would be futile.

I had been urged to dash back to school for a quick briefing from researchers at the University of Brighton, before going on to the next meeting. The researchers had been analysing the factors that seemed to deter parents from sending their children to the school. They just wanted to give me a quick overview of their findings.

Parental perceptions of East Brighton College of Media Arts: the slug

The survey findings were devastating: details are given as an Appendix on the Web site. The researchers asked children to identify their overall image of the College of Media Arts by comparing it and their first choice school with an animal.

First-Choice School: A tiger that is happy and playful but nothing else can eat. It can spring into action.

College of Media Arts: A slug — stupid, dirty and slimy but slowly getting better. Slow at education.

Despite everything we had done, nothing had changed in external perceptions. The research team made a number of recommendations, none of which were new. We were dealing with a depth of prejudice so profound that it would be years before any real difference would be made; and years we patently did not have because the deficit was mounting so fast. The PFI contract would only make matters worse because we would have to pay for facilities whether or not we had students on roll.

Much later, I discovered how unlikely it was that the College of Media Arts project would ever succeed. Anthony Edkins, the head of Falmer High School, had heard from the Director of Education who had set up the Fresh Start that she never expected it to succeed. When Phil Revell, the *TES* journalist, interviewed officers of the Council he discovered an amazing resentment that I had got the school out of Special Measures. I had not been expected to do so. It is only now that I realize I had joined the scapegoat community more thoroughly than I had ever expected.

I did not return to Hove for a meeting related to the Faith schools initiative. There was another PFI meeting to attend, and then an emergency governors' meeting about the disclosure to the press. I left the school at about eight o'clock and drove home like an automaton. The cats climbed on to my lap and a professional colleague rang. He had been prepared to drive some hundreds of miles to spend a few hours with me because he knew how dreadful the situation was, and wanted to express solidarity, offer advice and help. I made an unprecedented decision, for me. I could not go into school tomorrow — not even to meet someone I deeply respected. Everything ached. I thought, 'I've stopped. I've just stopped.'

I went to my doctor for a routine appointment, already twice cancelled.

The doctor was new to me. We went through the usual routine. 'Fine,' he said. 'Is there anything else?' Ten minutes later I was on my way out of the surgery in a state of shock. 'I am sending you home for four weeks, *in the first instance,*' in a tone of particular emphasis. 'You don't need any medication other than rest.'

There were two weeks until the end of term; but I went home as directed. In the course of our conversation, the doctor volunteered the fact that he used to be the school doctor in East Brighton. 'I know the children on Whitehawk. When they're five, they're still fine. By the time they're eight, they're angry.' I thought they were probably angry by the age of five.

In January 2003, just before the start of the new term, I went back to see the doctor. 'No, you aren't ready yet,' drawing the pad towards him to write out another note for sick leave. 'What did I write last time? *Acute exhaustion brought on by unreasonable workload.* You may never go back, you know.' I felt I was betraying the students for whom I wanted so much to make a difference; but the atmosphere of disbelief was now exactly what it had been when first I arrived. I did not know how to find the energy to start again. I had ignored the warnings of family and friends for the past several months, although I saw their distress. I had unintentionally shut everyone else out as I concentrated on the school. Now there was no choice at all. 'You are suffering from grief,' the doctor said. 'These are the signs of mourning.'

Although I love what I now do, everything has changed. Someone said to me a few months ago, 'I always wondered if you were arrogant or naïve. I think you were naïve, probably.' I don't think so; I had just decided to try to put my energy where my ideals were; always a risk.

What I do now

Whilst on sick leave I struggled hard with a sense of betrayal: if I returned, I would betray my family and friends who had repeatedly said, 'You are killing yourself.' If I did not return I would betray the students. Eventually I came to understand that there was really no choice if I wanted to use my wits as I had hoped, to try to make a real difference in children's lives. I could have returned, to the same unremitting work, and still made very little difference at all, because I would be unable to influence the social forces that made these students and their families into scapegoats. I thought that if I were working with street children in Calcutta then the situation would be different, but Brighton was an affluent, attractive and extremely self-confident community. It had no right to condemn some of its children to life as outsiders. I had made no impact on the Admissions policy, on parental perceptions, on the balance of dysfunctional students in the school. No one would attend to what I might say because I too was now marginalized. I tried to imagine the situation with a different headteacher, with more skills than I had; but on the other hand, I was the one who was prepared to try.

For a couple of months I did little but wrestle with my own demons. Then I began the slow process of unlearning headship — or rather transforming what I had felt and experienced into a capacity to see and understand the experiences of other school leaders. I embarked on the process of becoming a consultant, to use what I had learned in a different forum. Consultancy does not mean filling other people with your ideas, but in some way emptying yourself, as you try to discover how you can help others to understand the meaning and direction of *their* experience.

More specifically, I was not prepared to give up the College of Media Arts battle. Instead of trying to work through personal leadership I have been seeking to locate some of the external pressures that create and sustain scapegoat communities, and to work with other people who have identified the same issue in society.

I have a rich life of a different kind, now. I work within the framework of the National College for School Leadership as a facilitator in a programme called New Visions, for headteachers in their early years of headship. It is a great privilege to listen to such passionate and thoughtful people meditating on the nature of their work.

The Secondary Heads Association has a significant programme of professional development for its members and others who wish to join, and I act as consultant and trainer in several of these, from helping governors to appoint headteachers, to working with all the staff in a school on a specific issue; or sometimes to working with staff from clusters of schools in an area.

I act as consultant to a federation of schools in the South Lakes — one which embraces a college of further education and a special school as well as several very successful secondary schools. The particular joy of this is being with staff who are not headteachers and rediscovering the directness with which they speak. No one tells the truth to their own headteacher — not so much from a desire to conceal but because of what happens in institutional life. Telling the truth in organizations is taxing.

Above all, from being a Trustee of The Grubb Institute I am now a core member of its staff, working with people whose disciplines embrace experience of working with public and private sectors; the judiciary; the prison service; primary care trusts; large and small corporations; education; churches; local and national groups; international companies. In all our work is the same desire: to help people identify their core place and purpose in society. Everything I now do is subsumed into this framework. I have moved outside the boundary of the school into the complex realities which exert pressure on schools. In a troubled way I recognize that without having been so badly hurt by the experience of trying to raise standards at East Brighton College of Media Arts I could not work as I now do. I did not intend this; but I accept it.

Chapter 10

Brave New World

I look back on my contrasting experiences of schools in the independent and maintained sectors, and feel how straightforward some aspects of education can be. I see that schools are required to take responsibility for what they cannot control. We set up systems called 'education', 'health', 'employment' or other such obvious categories, in order to try to manage the complexities of social behaviour; but each of us experiences these systems through our own unique consciousness. What we struggle with is our sense of mutual accountability — or lack of it. Are all human beings equal, or are some, as expressed by George Orwell, in *Animal Farm*, more equal than others? Do our systems ensure that some people's judgements and experiences are less valid than other people's?

Getting out of Special Measures is straightforward.

Getting out of Special Measures.

The steps are simple enough:

- Find out what standards of achievement students have reached, and what affects this.

- Be clear about how teachers relate to students — not just in lessons but in every other context in the school; and build the relationships between teachers and students.

- Be analytical and precise in all your plans.

- Help everyone to hope and trust, and be full of hope and trust yourself. Live with other people's failings unless they damage students' hopes.

- Ask repeatedly how you know what you know about almost anything: what is happening in the classrooms and outside them; what students and staff think and feel; what work is going on.

- Look for evidence everywhere, and record it: respectful behaviour not just to adults, but between peers (at one level it may be as simple as willingness to apologize); improvements in work books (again, it may be as small as the ability to write in paragraphs for two sides of paper instead of crude sentences for half a page); exciting teaching which another adult has seen and evaluated; plans made and then carried out, watched carefully, appreciated, modified.

- Tell everyone how well they do.

- If things go wrong, blame last; look first at how systems may inadvertently undermine or work against success; and explain what you are doing.

But all that this achieves is a certain kind of political correctness within the education system.

Politics and education: the temptation

Schools are the subject of intense political scrutiny for several reasons:

- People remember from their own schooldays the influence and authority of that experience.
- They expect schools to ensure that young people acquire skills and qualifications to use in adult life so that society stays stable and predictable.
- They believe that investment in the young is investment in the future — in some concept of progress and improvement

Politicians focus on schools, because schools have huge social influence. Parents focus on schools because they start out as partners in bringing up children and eventually become powerful competitors for adolescent attention.

If you ask the average teenager who is most influential in his or her life, s/he will usually refer to a friendship group. Probe more deeply and you will often be told, 'My mum.' The influence of parents is primary; but schools are not far behind because they are densely populated by potential friendship groups, or gangs, and by interested and interesting adults, who also want to put children first. If young people do not find they are able to 'belong' to their school, they will find a substitute in another group of similar age — whether a street gang, a football club or another association. The artful work of the school is to provide a safe place for learning how to grow up, both individually and in the group.

At the highest level, the group becomes the team, and powerful collective learning takes place where both teachers and students play a full part. The school creates a culture which gives young people an insight into the kind of society they want to join or to create.

At its worst, however, the school replicates the experience of parents who do not challenge or question their own assumptions about life, and whose aspirations for their children are not different from their hopes for themselves. Ironically, this is a description not only of some of our obviously worst schools — the failing schools in inner cities and rural corners — but of the coasting middle-class schools in leafy suburbs.

The difference is this: where the latter are independent schools, they are likely to close; where they are state schools, they are likely to drift along, because articulate middle-class children will meet parental expectation regardless of schooling.

The fallibility of examination results

The examination results in such schools are likely to fit the Bell curve of average distribution of intelligence. Everyone will agree that because there is a concept of 'average' some will climb above it, and some will fall beneath. The prevailing tone of the debate about standards is based on the assumption that there must be ever more refined ways of discriminating, through assessment, so that you can detect who are 'the best and the brightest'. Universities complain that it is hard to differentiate between levels of A grade at Advanced level because they want evidence that can be perceived as reliable in order to reject candidates. People are suspicious of the concept that intelligence improves, although recent evidence is that IQ scores have increased during the last thirty years.

Never assume that what is presented by students is the real face of their learning/experience. They have deep knowledge and experience which is quite independent of school, and these may be far more powerful drivers than anything encountered at school, however good the school or intelligent the student. They only spend 9% of their lives in school each year. The task of the school is to engage this learning and experience, not to set it aside.

Incompetent or poor behaviour in students probably arises when the student is asked to perform within an inadequate or poor system. Most students want to please and to do well. Those who do not are usually deeply damaged. Before deciding to blame someone, look first to the system. This may need radical review. The curriculum may just be deeply boring. Where someone shows a high level of skill but is unable to write about it or explain it, there must still be an underlying intelligence, deserving respect, and necessary in a complete society.

There is real confusion about what it means to grow up, especially if it is suggested that people can become more 'intelligent' as a result of experience. Yet independent schools have to work on this assumption, even though they rarely say this. They work with the concept 'no pupil can be allowed to fail' because that is the market in which they operate.

Can 'success' be infectious?

Independent schools seem to be successful in producing both powerful social networks and well-qualified young people. With 7% of schools still providing at least 40% of the student population at Oxbridge, and filling the top places in league tables, politicians seem to have been convinced that the independent school model, as they understand it, is one to follow. 'Raising the standards of all to the standards of the best' assumes that 'best' is high qualification and social confidence.

So some obvious characteristics of independent schools can now be found in maintained schools:

- There is much more money available (but still not at the same level, and still not given wholly into the control of governors).
- There is competition between schools (collaboration is talked of, but is almost impossible to sustain in the presence of league tables and externally controlled admissions).
- Parental preference is given priority.

These are some of the consequences:

- The discrepancy between schools judged to be 'good' and 'failing' has become greater than ever.
- 'Good' schools are directed to expand, whether or not they have the facilities, and regardless of the impact of changing size upon a school's ethos.

- Schools in 'challenging circumstances' are very unlikely to be seen as desirable or to be rated as 'good' by the marketplace, whatever inspectors say.

- The state sector is dishonest in its recruitment. It requires schools to be inclusive (the successor to 'comprehensive') whilst colluding with whatever market forces seem to prevail at the time. It rejects social engineering whilst allowing unintentional or uncoordinated social engineering to dictate the shape and nature of schools. Schools in the state sector can rapidly fail, having once been successful. Why?

Other factors favouring independent schools:

- Most independent schools are significantly smaller than state schools. Independent schools that become over-large are usually criticised by parents as too commercially orientated. Parents prefer small classes, in institutions where children and adolescents are well known and recognized. The honest market relationship allows schools to determine their own size, their own fees, and their own nature.

- It is hard to run a small school well because of the economic pressures it endures, and yet a small school is as likely to be as highly effective as a large school. State schools are unable to regulate their own size directly: compare the indicative intake number with the real intake number year after year to see how schools can be overruled by external appeals tribunals as to the number of children they must accept.

- Independent schools largely recruit through the ability of parents to pay fees. Recruitment for ability is only possible at times, and for some schools. In times of recession, independent schools take whomever they can get; but their results are expected to stay the same. They usually do. Why?

Characteristics of independent schools which contribute to their success

1. Control over money

Independent schools have direct and total control of their fees and all financial processes.

2. Decision-making

Governors and head together make all the decisions, restricted simply, though considerably, by all the legislation that relates to children, the workplace, employment rights, financial and other codes of practice, and the rules of the Charities Commission. That still leaves a lot of room for manoeuvre.

3. Expectations

Independent schools forge contracts with parents for the payment of fees. The client is therefore formally the parent; but most schools would consider the pupil to be the client on whose behalf the parent is negotiating. The underlying contract between school and pupil is that the school will use every tool it can find to make sure that the pupil feels both happy and successful — because otherwise the parents will remove the child from the school.

4. Freedom to decide

As head of an independent school, I was free to make all sorts of decisions, many of which I have already described. I was directly accountable to parents and governors, and always encouraged pupils to speak up, so I was hardly likely to made foolish decisions. Invariably I consulted widely and worked with consensus — but where necessary, I stuck my neck out.

5. Freedom to fit education to the pupils' needs

Schools ought to provide safe places for the would-be learner to attempt fantastically ambitious projects as well as routine and mundane tasks. There is no escaping the boringly tedious tasks that frequent adult life, so one might as well learn in school how to set one's mind to deal with these. But at the same time, school offers a wonderfully positive place in which to try out the skills which adults outside the school are likely to inhibit, for a variety of reasons. It is not difficult, using the leverage of being a school, to introduce pupils to a huge range of opportunities that the individual parent will never be able to facilitate.

6. Freedom to be creative

There is usually an excellent correlation between the access to rich opportunities, both through the curriculum and in extra-curricular activities, and examination results, whatever the child's abilities seem to be. The abilities grow in response to the stimuli given. There is plenty of research evidence to support this.

It is a good starting place in an education system. You try to sense and develop the child's own sense of excellence; you say that it matters; you encourage practice; you use all your ingenuity to ensure that the environment is richly creative. The school is well placed to recognize and reward the aptitude and the practice; it is uniquely placed in its capacity to create a 'real' world: a bounded place with rules, codes, expectations and a culture in which that aptitude can be exercised in relation to others. School is or can be another form of game.

Of course, these opportunities also exist in state schools, but in a culture where teaching hours are counted, where health and safety issues inculcate caution, where booster classes and homework clubs attract separate funding, where teachers are under pressure continually to revise their lesson plans in the light of yet another strategy, and where the alternative curriculum is primarily devised for the disaffected. I have not yet encountered a state school with the richness and depth of extra-curricular provision that most independent schools offer, that creates an alternative curriculum which any pupil can access, at any level.

7. Generous resources

The average classroom teacher in an independent school probably teaches for about 75% or 80% of each week. The rest of their time is not necessarily free — but they will have the time and, more importantly, the energy and motivation to work creatively with pupils at projects which pupils choose for themselves. This means that at any break, or lunchtime, or after school on any day of the week, there will be many adults out and about with pupils. At its simplest, pupils can see a wide variety of adult behaviours, and choose to relate to or imitate any number. They also see many of their peers equally engaged and purposeful, regardless of the time of day.

Creativity, culture and education: independent and maintained schools compared

'All Our Futures: Creativity, Culture and Education' was a remarkable publication that the DfES produced and then ignored. Creativity is back on the political/educational agenda again, but the systems for supporting it are hard to find. These comparisons highlight factors that cramp creativity in maintained schools.

1. Self-governing

Independent schools are self-governing. Who makes decisions is entirely clear.

In maintained schools, the boundary of governance is blurred: LEA as the arm of the political local council as the arm of the political DfES. Governors have legal responsibilities for the budget, for appointments, for policies of all kinds — but they are volunteers with authority and very little power. The LEA can and does blame the DfES; and vice versa. Who makes decisions is not clear.

2. Known budget, managed autonomously

Independent schools know from the outset how much money will be available to them and do not have to account to anyone except the parents and the Charities Commission for how that money is spent.

Maintained schools rarely know how much their total budget will be; they are often in the situation of being told to spend money on specific priorities regardless of whether or not the funds exist. They have to bid into and account to a number of different funding streams and although these have recently been simplified, headteachers often waste huge amounts of time and energy trying to meet one aim, only to discover either that the resources do not exist or that some other agency, the real budget-holder, has mismanaged.

3. Tailored curriculum

Independent schools are free to determine the curriculum and teaching that best fits their students. There is still some dull teaching in independent schools, relying far too much on the compliance of the student population; but staff have time enough not just to develop good relationships with students but to work alongside them in activities which students choose — a sort of alternative curriculum, which is usually very rich and varied. Students become good learners because they are given plenty of opportunities to learn rather than to be instructed.

Creativity has been squeezed out of the maintained system quite relentlessly over the last twenty years. There is some outstandingly good teaching to be found in these schools, and a passion for improvement, but staff are forever having to adjust to yet another initiative, yet another strategy, yet another direction imposed from outside. There is virtually no time for schools to generate the energy, the initiative and the strategy from within.

4. Direct contract between school and parents

The contract is directly between the parents and the school, for the benefit of the child. No one else is involved. The knack of the recruiting headteacher in the independent sector is to make every child feel s/he has been chosen for this school — even if budget constraints mean the child will be accepted regardless.

In the maintained system, who decides on how children are allocated to schools is not clear. Schools claim to be directed by local education authorities, who say that they are told by government what to do, which says it is answerable to voters who want freedom to choose — and those voters find themselves often caught in systems as mysterious as a maze. Only a few seem to hold the thread.

5. No child can be allowed to fail

Overwhelmingly, the idea that dominates independent school culture is: no child can be allowed to fail. This is a straightforward response to market forces. Both pupils and staff are motivated by the urge to fulfil the predication that 'students at this school do very well'. There can be no acceptance of the term 'average'.

Maintained schools use data very strictly to predict results at the different key stages. They try to make these aspirational, too; but all the schools I know assume that if the measured ability of an intake drops, then the predicted outcomes will drop. So schools can and do predict that results for certain sets of pupils will be lower than for others.

6. Parental influence

In independent schools, the influence of parents is openly recognized. league tables confirm the significance of parental commitment, expectation and input. To those who have, more will be given.

Students whose parents cannot and will not accept the importance of education have suffered from the outset. Although additional resources are sometimes provided for these students, they are not usually of the kind most urgently and profoundly needed: exceptionally talented and skilled other adults, who can help to compensate for the absence of good parents and the distortion to brain development that this absence entails. Anyone who believes that I have grossly exaggerated the situation should consult the research findings. (*Meaningful Differences in the Everyday Experiences of Young American Children* Hart and Risley 1995; and *The Social World of Children Learning to Talk* Hart and Risley 1999.)

What schools cannot control

American researchers Betty Hart and Todd Risley worked for many years to analyse the ways in which parents interact with their children in the first three or four years of life. They wanted to see whether or not *class* is related to intelligence and achievement. They gathered an enormous database of evidence from the families of professionals, the working-class, and the welfare class, logging the spoken interactions between parents and children as *encouragements* and *discouragements*.

The evidence published in these two books is stark: our measures of intelligence are probably entirely related to class, because parents talk to children in ways that will prepare them for lives such as their own. Hart and Risley discovered that by the time the child of the professional reaches the age of 3, s/he will have experienced 700,000 encouragements and 80,000 discouragements. The welfare child, on the other hand, will have experienced 60,000 encouragements and 120,000 discouragements. The child of professional parents will have heard 50 million words by the time s/he is 4 years old; the welfare child will only have heard 12 million. The 3-year-old child of professionals has a larger vocabulary than the adult in the welfare system.

Hart and Risley did not judge that professional parents loved their children more than welfare parents; on the contrary, they discovered that welfare parents were preparing their children for the lives of unassuaged poverty that they themselves lived. They thought it was their duty: children would have to follow orders when they grew up, because they would have menial work, or none. They taught the appropriate vocabulary and transactions to their infant children.

Hart and Risley call it 'transgenerational poverty.' (The American attempt to remedy this situation has influenced our SureStart scheme.) They calculated that the experience of the welfare child could be made equal to that of a working-class child, if 41 hours a week of additional experience 'as rich in words addressed to the child as that in an average professional home' could be provided (p205). They thought that a further 40 hours per week of 'substituted experience' would be needed for the ratio of encouragement to discouragement to be put right. Although this research is American, there is every reason to believe that a similar situation exists here. I saw it in East Brighton.

What next?

State schools are like sieves leaking expertise, energy and talent. There is nothing wrong with the staff in state schools, or the ideas they generate. What stifles them is the political system which pressurizes them to conform instead of to respond directly to the students and their parents. Given some of the freedoms, disciplines and expectations outlined above — and transformed social systems — they would be every bit as successful as independent schools in making sure that every child succeeds.

Current ways of predicting results and setting targets have the same validity as predicting that the quality of apples will be worse next year because of this year's drought. We would expect the farmer to protect water supply for the apple orchard, or the physiotherapist to plan an exercise programme for someone with a broken leg. We could plan to improve the living and learning environment for the pupils predicted to fall short. This is what the independent sector does. And I have seen this done spectacularly well in an Early Years Centre, so I know that it is possible. Schools which truly practise inclusion have to change assumptions at an absolutely fundamental level: the level of belief in what 'ability' and 'intelligence' actually are, and to what extent schools alone can make the difference.

In state schools that serve healthy communities, there is no reason for failure. The whole community supports the school; school is a microcosm of society. Any deficiencies in such schools simply mirror society. The recurrent complaint about disaffection in young people is a fine example because we still tend to think of children and young people as in need of our care and attention, rather than engaging with them so that they are able to grow up. We are child-focused rather than child-centred; too often, demonstrations of power by young people are perceived as highly threatening, instead of as healthy attempts to discover the strengths they must learn to survive in an unpredictable future.

Our current political system forces schools to compete with one another for pupils so that the schools cannot be single-mindedly committed to education. Schools actually possess huge intellectual capital and could provide tremendous insight into the factors which affect social function — they could provide wonderful advice — but they are effectively neutered by this unnecessary competitive distraction.

Independent schools compete, set up systems for competition, and are wholly in charge of the business of education. All the boundaries are clear and have long been so. They are, of course, utterly divisive social institutions, but as long as society legislates for people to use their personal resources to buy facilities, then they have the same rights to operate as any other business. In consequence, independent schools have developed sophisticated relationships with the parents and communities from which their students come. Of course, if those businesses fail there are state schools for pupils to attend instead.

But for the most fragile people there should surely be no such reliance on free market forces. Adults may choose to become vulnerable (which I doubt), but children are most certainly born innocent in this regard.

Choices

The desires represented in the two most recent Children Acts suggest a bringing to the surface of some of our inconsistent feelings about vulnerable children. We do not like, and want to avoid, dysfunctional adults. We have set up systems for so-called integration of vulnerable children into the mainstream, but have woefully muddled up different categories of dysfunction. A wheel-chair-bound or partially hearing child who comes from a loving and well-balanced home is already part of the mainstream, whether or not they attend school with everyone else.

The truly vulnerable are brought up on the margins. We know that intelligence is not determined by postcode: in principle. In practice, we let postcodes create intelligence, because social experience is a mighty power in determining how brains and moral awareness develop. We now well understand how infants grow up seriously damaged by the experiences of their parents and community.

We could begin to address this by honestly getting to grips

with the postcode itself. Postcodes are geographical areas. Wherever a school is struggling because there are so many challenging pupils to manage, the first step should be to disperse those children to other schools to make sure that on a day-to-day basis they experience being part of a healthy community. In small towns, there are rarely problems because the integration is complete. If, however, the small town is desolate because a major employer has disappeared, then all the social, emotional and financial problems experienced by the adults will instantly be seen in the school. The one cannot be separated from the other.

In cities where schools are compelled to compete, we need to look afresh at what is meant by 'community'. In the world of the Internet and widespread travel, it is nonsensical to pretend that 'community' means local neighbourhood alone: it means the area of belonging that the inhabitants of a geographical area are entitled to experience.

Plainly, dispersing children is a short-term expedient. The real area for concentration is on how communities are put together geographically: what's in the postcode? What makes a sustainable community?

Until we resolve this, we should be encouraging schools to deal creatively with the problems they find in their local communities. We should expect to fund them on widely different assumptions and to give them complete freedom of control over their budgets. Instead of talking glibly about encouraging 'bright' children from 'working-class backgrounds' to escape through aspiration into some El Dorado of higher education, we should be thinking clearly about how to use the latest research on how intelligence grows or is stunted, to redesign our social structures and assumptions. This is the evidence we should be using, not data-banks about Key Stage results which are largely records of current social structures. The Department for Education should be the Department for Human Development.

We should be searching for entirely different kinds of teachers: those with emotional maturity, willing to learn alongside the young so that children discover through experience the adults they could become. We don't need subject teachers. We can find subject coaches.

If we start looking honestly at the impulses we try to hide or justify — 'I don't want my child in school with children like that' — and at the circumstances which give rise to such feelings, we would discover how to enable every child to succeed. It will not be easy because most of us are still reluctant to redefine the circle of belonging. At present, our education system is politically adjusted to endorse failure. We use the scapegoat as a means of projecting all that we do not like about ourselves onto another, whom we send out into a desert, so that we can tell ourselves these aspects of human experience are nothing to do with us. Indeed, we seem to need scapegoats so that we can experience ourselves as more perfect than we really are. But if we want a peaceful, creative and just society, we have to accept that everyone belongs. There can be no outsiders.

Index

ALSO PUBLISHED BY UIT CAMBRIDGE LTD.

Leading Schools from Failure to Success

John Bazalgette,
Bruce Reed, Ian Kehoe and Jean Reed
The Grubb Institute

With a foreword by Lord Dearing

The book describes how three church schools were transformed from failing to over-subscribed, solely by appointing a new headteacher. The schools remained remained non-selective, and the nature of the pupil intake was unchanged.

The book emphasizes:

- What we want from education is not league table scores, but pupils who become well-adjusted adults ready to engage in society, while still achieving high academic standards.
- How the inclusiveness created by the heads' attitude to pupils fundamentally changed the school.
- How the religious background to a school's ethos benefits all pupils — of any or no faith. While all three headteachers in the case-studies were practising Christians, the book is predominantly neither faith- nor faith-school-specific.

This book is important for national and local policy-makers as well as teachers and parents, because it explains what succeeds in practice, *without* extra funding from LEA or Government.

ISBN: 0-9544529-2-5